Life Lessons of a Throwaway Kid

By Cordell Farley

Life Lessons of a Throwaway Kid

Publishing Consultant
The Pierce Agency, LLC, USA
www.ThePierceAgencyLLC.com
804.549.2884
Email: rebekah@thepierceagencyllc.com

Cover Design
Sassi Concepts & Designs, Inc.

Cover Image Courtesy of © Grandmaisonc | Dreamstime.com - US Cellular Baseball Field Photo

Printed in the U.S.A.
ISBN -13: 978-1507834213
ISBN -10: 1507834217

Cordell Farley

Acknowledgements

I would first like to thank my beautiful and loving wife, Latrice Farley. This book would not have been possible without her passion and strength in supporting me. She pushed and pulled things out of me that I had buried deep in my soul many years ago. I thank her for her persistence and her patience as she helped me create this memoir. I would also like to thank my children who have been awesome throughout this process. My story would not be my story without the people who raised me – to you I say thank you. Many thanks to my mentor and friend, Carl Vaughn, for his support in helping me to get this book published.

I would also like to thank Henry "Bug" Booker, Carol Booker, Andriea "Nikki" Hill, LaTasha Rasberry and Sharmaine Hobbs who took time out of their busy lives to read the original manuscript and provide critical feedback. A special thanks to Rebekah Pierce with The Pierce Agency for helping me shape and polish this memoir. Your skills and expertise were invaluable.

A final and last thank you to all of the coaches, teammates, and friends I encountered along my journey. You helped shape me into the person I am today. I am forever indebted to you.

3

Part I

Chapter 1 ~ Where It All Began

Summer 1977

BOOM!!!!! The deafening sound of the baseball cracking against my head rings loudly in my ears as I step off the last step into the backyard to play. I can feel myself falling, but I can't catch myself. As the fresh wet grass brushes against my face, I feel the warmth of something flowing down my leg.

Oh no! Did I just pee myself? Please don't let that be pee! I'm gonna be in so much trouble for messing up my clothes...ooh...I can't seem to keep my eyes open... DARKNESS...

****

*LIGHT...Ouch! The light is so bright as I squint to open my eyes. My head is pounding! Where **am** I? The hospital, maybe? What happened to me? I'm so afraid. Where is everybody? This is so weird; what am I doing in this bed? Wait a minute...I'm in bed...at home???!!! Boy, I must be really sick for Big Ma to let me sleep in the bed!! I wonder if I'm gonna die. Oh gosh! That must be it! God help me!*

Maybe I'm just dreaming...if it's a dream, I don't wanna wake up! This soft mattress and these cool pillows feel so much better than that hard, cold floor I'm used to sleeping on. I could get used to this! Oooh...I'm feeling woozy again...I...I can't keep my eyes open...DARKNESS

That moment is the first memory I have as a child. At four years old, I was cold-cocked in the head by a fast flying baseball thrown by one of the many kids playing in my backyard. I'm sure this is a memory that many kids have experienced. I'm also pretty sure that for most of those kids that memory also included a doting parent and something like milk and cookies to ease the pain. That type of memory would have been just a fairytale for me.

When I finally woke up from being knocked unconscious for who knows how long, I was in total shock just to be actually lying in a bed. I was so used to sleeping on the floor that the comforting feeling of the bed was one I wanted to hold onto for as long as I could. My head was throbbing and pounding like a little drummer boy wailing on his drum, but none of that mattered at the very moment. The only thing that mattered was that for once I felt like a regular little boy lying in that bed.

My mom, or Big Ma as she was known to most in the neighborhood, must have been feeling rather generous that day because somehow I had miraculously avoided getting my butt torn out the frame for peeing on myself AND she let me get in the bed. I think getting knocked out must have scared her. Ok, well, obviously not enough to take me to a hospital, but long enough to let me lie in the bed for a couple of hours! I was on cloud nine; it didn't matter that it wouldn't last.

To make things a little clearer, I lived in one of the biggest foster homes in the small town of Blackstone, Virginia. It certainly wasn't big in physical size; it was a doublewide trailer with four small bedrooms, two bathrooms (one of which was strictly for Big Ma's use only), a den turned quasi bedroom, a medium-sized living room, a small dining room that was also used sometimes as a temporary bedroom, and, of course, a kitchen. It was, however, big in terms of how many people lived there at any given moment. I wasn't a foster child, or so I thought at the time, but almost everyone else that lived there was and there were plenty of them.

Big Ma, the head of our household, only stood about 5 feet tall (at best), but her round, stocky stature and stern demeanor made her seem as if she were about

8 feet tall. She had a beautiful brown shade of skin and hair as black as coal. She had stunning brown eyes that were cold and seemed to speak their own language. She commanded any room she was in and most everyone, adults and children alike, had a mix of reverence and fear for her. If I could give a visual and mental description of her, it would be a cross between the character "Sophia," played by Oprah Winfrey from *The Color Purple*, and "Vera," the character played by Della Reese in *Harlem Nights.*

Granddaddy (that's what everyone called my dad), on the other hand, had a completely different demeanor and approach to all of the foster kids that roamed around in the house. He stood nearly 6 feet tall, but his lanky features and demure stature made him look much smaller. If there is one main phrase I could use to describe him from the viewpoint of a kid it would be quiet and distant, so much so that it was almost as if he wasn't there. He certainly walked lightly around Big Ma and we never heard him raise his voice. He worked, he cooked and he watched TV.

Big Ma was Nottoway County Social Services Department's "go to" person for foster care. If a child needed a place to stay, our house was always open, and I do mean ALWAYS. I believe if speed dial would have existed back then, our phone number would have been number one. It didn't matter when they came either. It could be in the middle of the day or it could be in the middle of the night. Sometimes they stayed for months and sometimes they stayed for years. Other times, it would be maybe for only one night. For example, let's say someone was stopped by the police and arrested for drunk driving, and their kids were in the car. The parents would go to lockup for the night and their kids would come to OUR lock-up…I mean house for the night. We never knew who or how many would come in at any given time. So to say that there was constant chaos in the house would be an understatement.

To add to that chaos, Big Ma and Granddaddy not only took in foster kids, but they also ran an informal nursing home of sorts. If an elderly person needed somewhere to stay AND they got a monthly disability or social security check, my parents would happily take them in. Many of them also had mental disabilities ranging from schizophrenia to bi-polar disorder, although back then I don't think they really had those "fancy" names for them. I just knew most of them got a "crazy" check and I tried to keep my distance, which really didn't work out most of the time. I could often hear them pacing up and down the road late at night talking to themselves or knocking on the windows to the trailer asking for cigarettes. I guess my parents had tried to separate them from us, but with the dynamic of the layout of the property, that really didn't work out too well.

The foster kids stayed in the house and the "crazy" people stayed in little "shacks" that my father had built on the lots adjacent to the trailer. And the shacks were just that: shacks! They sat just off to the right of our trailer on our lot. There were about seven shacks in all as well as two smaller trailers and two small houses that also sat on the two acre lot. The two smaller trailers and houses actually had multi-use purposes. Sometimes they were rented out and sometimes we used them for the elderly residents; it just depended on the situation and the funds that went along with it. All I knew was that there were a lot of people everywhere all the time.

How Big Ma and Granddaddy managed to juggle between dozens of foster kids and dozens of elderly people all at once truly escapes me, but it was a lucrative business for them that put food on the table for us. Who was I to judge? I was just glad that there were always a lot of people in the house. And although this may seem strange, having all those people around actually helped me out.

Big Ma always seemed to have a lot of negative energy directed towards me and having other people in the house helped buff some of it. It felt as if I, at four years old, was the bane of her existence. No matter what or who was irking her at any given time, it seemed as if I always caught the brunt of her ire and it was never pretty. Even if one of the other kids had done something, she would somehow direct the energy towards me – normally with putting me to work. She seemed dissatisfied if I were not constantly doing something in regards to chores or housework. It could be anything from getting clothes off the line to taking food trays to the old people that lived in the shacks on the side of the house. The worst of them would be cleaning out the dog pens – and there were plenty of dogs to clean up after.

As soon as I finished one chore, she would immediately direct me to the next one. If I didn't finish in the time she felt it should have taken me, she would berate me by calling me "dumb" and "stupid." This would normally be followed by a threat to put me in what she referred to as "the crazy house" or send me to Crossroads, a mental health facility. I didn't exactly know what either meant at the time, but I knew it wasn't anything that would be pleasant based on the context and fervor with which she would spew these warnings at me. I could only relate "crazy house" to the same people, who I mentioned earlier that walked around talking to themselves or screamed obscenities at any given time to no one in particular. I didn't talk to myself (at least not out loud, anyway) and I certainly didn't walk around screaming and cussing, so why did she constantly compare me to them? I was only trying to be a good boy. That really wasn't good enough, I guess. Every time she directed those threats at me, they scared me to death.

Chapter 2 One Big "Family"

Big Ma ruled the house with an iron fist. She didn't take anything off of anyone – especially Granddaddy. In retrospect, I guess she really had no choice in order to keep any kind of order in a house full of kids that weren't biologically hers. At any given time, there would be anywhere from 10-15 people living in that small, four bedroom double-wide trailer. That included me, my Big Ma, Granddaddy, my sister Mary, my Uncle Willy, several cousins, my three teenage nieces – who were much older than me - and, of course, all of the foster kids.

Mary was one year older than me and she was the apple of Granddaddy's eye. She could do no wrong. My nieces were my other older sister's daughters. She was almost 30 years older than me and was already out on her own and married with five kids - four girls and one boy - by the time I was born. I really don't know how it came to be or under what circumstances, but by the time they were teenagers, the three older girls had moved in with us. They were the apple of Big Ma's eye and she would have done, and did do, any and everything for them.

Uncle Willy was Big Ma's brother. He was an Army veteran who never got married or had kids. He had fought in one of the wars (I don't recall which one) and that experience had definitely taken a toll on him. He was a quiet alcoholic that would sometimes leave for months at a time and then just show back up, but Big Ma would always take him back in. I was always thrilled to see him after such long absences because I always felt good when he was around. When he was home, we always stayed in the same room or space (whichever was available). When he wasn't drunk, he would actually take the time to talk to me like I was a real human being. I was ecstatic when he would send me to the store to buy him the Sir Walter Raleigh bags of tobacco for his pipe (this, of course, was when I was old enough to buy them, which back then meant you were old enough if you could see over the counter). Although those moments with Uncle Willy were rare, I cherished them.

As I said before, Granddaddy didn't say much at all. He just seemed to go along with the flow – whatever Big Ma said, he pretty much went with it. He knew better than to cross her, although at the time, I sometimes wondered why he didn't. Truthfully, no one in town ever really crossed her except her two neighbors who both lived about three football fields from us on the same street. They were two women who were almost just as feisty as my mom and they didn't have a problem going toe-to-toe with her, although, technically, it was from the safety of their porches. They would get into these epic shouting matches that could be heard throughout the entire neighborhood. They never dared come onto her property to confront her, though; they were much smarter than that.

Big Ma ran a tight ship in her home and anyone that stepped out of line would feel her wrath. Whatever was closest to her at the moment was what went upside your head. It didn't matter if it was a belt, a rope, an extension cord, a switch, an ashtray, or a shoe; if it was near her and you got out of line, she was coming for you. If you weren't within physical reach that was quite okay because the sharpness of her tongue could cut deeper than a knife and inflict much more damage than any belt or rope could ever hope to.

At one point, I was convinced that my God-given name was "Dummy." I seemed to have a special gift for pissing her off. I was quiet and tried to stay out of the way, but that didn't seem to work. It was as if just the sight of me would send her into a rage. I began to think that her disdain towards me was because I was born a boy. She had my two sisters, all these grand girls and

11

then she had me – a rambunctious, little curly-headed boy. She was already 44 by the time I was born, so her patience probably wasn't what it maybe once was either.

I was further convinced that she had wanted a girl because of what she allowed my nieces to do to me. Every night, they dressed me in a pretty little nightgown before I went to bed and put curling rollers and girly bows in my hair. They all thought it was "cute." They never even got in trouble for it.

As for Mary, like I said, she could do no wrong – whatever she wanted, she got. She even had her own room. Only four bedrooms in the entire house, all these people living there, and she didn't have to share it with a soul! Well, she did end up sharing it with her 17-year-old boyfriend when she was around 12 years old, but that was her choice and no one seemed to think anything was wrong with it. I didn't care about any of that, though. I just wanted some space to myself in the midst of the constant chaos and the peace of not always fearing I would be yelled at.

At five years old, I had already begun to pray to God about all my "troubles." Big Ma insisted we go to Sunday school and church every first and second Sunday, so I had already learned that God was supposed to be my protector. I had found a little place out by a big empty field to the left of our trailer where I would often go to pray. "This too shall pass" is what I would repeatedly say while on my knees in that empty field. While I didn't fully understand the concept of what it truly meant, I knew it had to relate to what I was going through and what I was feeling. I knew things would get better, but I just didn't know when. Unfortunately for me, the "when" would be a long time coming.

Chapter 3 ~ The Perfect Prey:
What's Done in the Dark Doesn't Always
Come to Light

Summer 1980 – Age 7

*DARKNESS... "Mann, wake up! Come with me,"
she whispered. "Come get in the bed with me."*

*Huh?? What?? Why is my 13-year-old foster
sister waking me up at 3am in the morning? What's
going on? I'm so tired from all the fun we had at the
skating rink earlier tonight...why is she waking me up
now of all times? Furthermore, why is she asking me to
get into bed with her? Maybe Big Ma sent her to tell me
get into bed because it's really cold tonight and the
hardwood floor in the den is especially cold...well no,
that doesn't make sense because the floor is even colder
in the winter and nobody ever bothers to wake me up. Oh,
well! I don't really care because this will be my first
chance to sleep in the bed since I got hit in the head a
couple of years ago. The bed is much warmer than the
floor...Ahh! Nice cool sheets...for once I can get a good
night's sleep...*

*"Mann, take your clothes off and get on top of
me," she said in a whisper.*

Wait...what did she just say?

*"Mann, TAKE YOUR CLOTHES OFF AND GET
ON TOP OF ME!!" she said a little firmer and a tad bit
louder.*

*I am not a baby that needs to be rocked to sleep,
so why do I need to get on top of her and why in the world
do I need to take my clothes off?*

"Do it now, come on," she says.

*This doesn't feel right, but I think I better listen
to her before she wakes somebody up...I don't wanna get*

in trouble with Big Ma...Oh no...she's touching my privates! Why is she doing that? I think I'm gonna be sick to my stomach...Noooo...why is she kissing me in my mouth??...Yuck!! I don't think she's supposed to be doing this...

Who told her she could do this to me? Maybe this is some type of punishment from Big Ma...no, she would never do that...Please, somebody wake up and tell her to stop! My stomach is hurting so bad I think I'm gonna throw up! Please somebody wake up...somebody wake up! I don't wanna do this!! She's grinding on my privates and it really hurts...I wanna scream, but I'm so scared. Big Ma is gonna be so mad if I wake everybody up...please let this be over...please let this be over...please, God, make it stop!!!

****

"Hey, Mann...come here...come get some yogurt. You know Big Ma not gonna let you have none. Don't you wanna taste it? I know you do...come on and lick some off the spoon...taste good, doesn't it?"

Oh man, this is good!! I'm glad somebody thinks I'm special enough to have some yogurt. She is so cool! This new foster sister is not too bad. She's sixteen, but she's been really nice to me since she moved in with us. Maybe I'll finally have an ally in this house.

"Mann, did you enjoy the yogurt? Good...now hold still while I pull down your pants."

What?? Why does she wanna pull down my pants? Maybe the yogurt is gonna give me diarrhea and she doesn't want me to mess my pants...she's so thoughtful... Whoa...why did she just put her mouth on my privates? That hurts!!! She is not nice! She is nasty!!! I don't like this game...where is everybody? Where is everybody? It's broad daylight!!

Why didn't I go outside to play when everybody else did? Ouch...my stomach hurts so bad! I wonder if

14

my other foster sister told her to do this. They are both so nasty! I hate them!!! Please, God, let this be over...I wanna scream so bad, but I'm scared...somebody please save me...God, please save me!

The vivid memories of my two teenage foster sisters violating me are forever etched into my brain. I was only 7 years old when they began molesting me. One of them would use the cloak of night to take advantage of me. She would wait until everyone was asleep and sneak into the den and command me to get in bed with her. At first, she would only do it occasionally, but once she figured out that I wasn't going to tell, it became routine.

The other one would wait until everybody would go outside and would use yogurt to get me to come to her. I'm sure that neither of them knew what the other was doing, but in my 7 year old brain, they had conspired with each other to torment me for their own personal, sick pleasure. I hated them so much, but instead of telling anyone, I just began to internalize it all.

In my mind, my parents should have sensed what was going on right under their noses, but then again with everything that was going on in the house and with so many people it would have been hard for them to know what was going on with each individual kid and elderly person. Maybe I deserved what was happening to me. I had been praying for attention and now I was getting it, so what could I say? This horrid thought process soon became my reality. I began to believe that every bad thing that happened to me was somehow my fault.

Chapter 4 ~ The Red House

Spring 1981 – Age 8

"What's 2x2?"
Four!!
"Good, now what's 3x2?"
Six!!…
"Faster! What's 4x5?"
Twenty!!
"Good job, Mann…now come on! Let's go play inside the red house."

The red house…it wasn't even a house, but that's what we called it. This small shack of sorts sat on one of the lots beside our trailer alongside the other seven shacks and two trailers. It looked like a cross between a house and an outdoor shed. Unlike a shed, though, there were dividers on the inside that made it look like rooms inside of a house. There were also hallowed out areas in each "room" that looked like windows should have been in them. And, of course, it was red.

Big Ma used it as a place to store all of the extra clothes and junk that she would get from yard sales. I forgot to mention earlier that Big Ma was a yard sale junkie. She faithfully headed out in the early hours every Saturday morning and would hit pretty much every yard sale in town. She would come back in the afternoons, the back of our big brown station wagon loaded down with everything from clothes and shoes to toys and just plain junk. All of us would run to the car like moths to a flame to rummage through all of the goodies she had returned with. It was like Goodwill on wheels! My foster brother Randy, who was the same age as me, would trade clothes back and forth and bargain with the other foster kids to get shoes that matched. It was every kid for himself. After we would finish our "shopping spree" in the station wagon, and our bargaining with the other kids, me and Randy would sit on the side of the trailer and daydream about what we were going be when we grew up. Randy was my other ally in the house, at least for the time that he was there. He was like a brother since I didn't have any of my own.

But back to the red house…whatever things we couldn't use or didn't want, Big Ma would just pile into the red house, and since she went to yard sales every week, the red house was overflowing with piles and piles of unwanted clothes. On warm days me, Mary, Randy and whatever foster kids were living with us at the time would sneak in, and jump around and around in the piles of old clothes. We had our very own jungle gym. It was so much fun – until it wasn't anymore.

Everything changed when a new girl and her schizophrenic mother moved into one of the houses on our property. She was 15 years old. For some reason, she took a special interest in wanting to help me with my math facts. I had already been held back in the first grade by Big Ma. She held me back because although I had struggled in science that year, my teacher was okay with promoting me to the second grade, that is, until she talked to Big Ma. I distinctly remember when the phone call came from the teacher near the end of the year. She presumably called to tell Big Ma that I would be getting promoted to the second grade. Big Ma sat quietly and listened to the teacher, and when she finished, Big Ma boldly uttered, "keep his a** in the first grade" and promptly hung up the phone. Although now a year behind, I was finally in the second grade. However, I was still struggling a bit in math. I most definitely did not want to be held back again, so I was more than eager for her to help me. Finally, someone was taking an interest in my school work. This was a first.

On the weekends, we would sit on the porch and she'd use flash cards to drill me on my facts. At one point, I was doing so well on my subtraction and addition that she began to teach me multiplication. This was fun, too – until it wasn't anymore. One Saturday, she told me that if I did well on my facts for the day she had a special treat just for me in the red house. She told me that no one else could see the treat, so I had to keep it a secret. I couldn't wait to see what my prize was inside of the red house! I whizzed through the drills and got every one of them right!

When we stepped, in I began to dig through the pile of clothes to look for my "special treat." To my dismay, I couldn't find it anywhere. As I continued to look around for the treat, I noticed she had sat down on a pile of clothes. She motioned for me to come sit next to her. Suddenly, before I knew it, she started kissing my neck and then she tried to kiss me in the mouth. I froze; I didn't know what to do. Without a second thought, she took my hands and put them in her pants. I went completely numb. I couldn't believe that this was happening yet again.

The touching and fondling went on for what felt like an eternity. I stood there motionless just wanting someone to walk in and save me. Like always, no one ever came. She began to make a habit out of this almost every weekend thereafter. And I didn't tell a soul. Who would care anyway?

Chapter 5 ~ The Race and John Gregory

Summer 1981 – Age 8

I had always enjoyed playing outside with other neighborhood kids, but after everything started happening with my foster sisters, my behavior began to change. I became withdrawn and I lost all confidence in everything I did. The adults didn't seem to notice, but other kids picked up on it like I had some kind of bull's eye on my head. It's as if they had some kind of special radar that allowed them to sniff out the weak and proceed to destroy. This is what began to happen to me. Suddenly, no one wanted me on their team anymore. I became *that* kid who always got picked last.

If we were playing pickup football, I wouldn't be allowed to stop playing until I scored a touchdown. The problem was my teammates never blocked for me. When we played baseball, we might as well have been playing a twisted version of football and kickball. The pitcher would take aim and fire off the ball directly at my head. Luckily for me, I had quick instincts and could avoid the direct hit and still hit the ball. The unfortunate part, though, is that as I rounded the bases, I was kicked, punched and shoved. Whether I was inside the house or outside, I couldn't seem to escape this living hell.

Ok, I'm gonna win this race...

I'm ready...

I'm gonna show everybody who I am...

"On your mark, get set, GO!!!!"

I open my eyes and sprint!! This is it...I'm gonna do it...I can do it...

I'm gonna win this race and show everybody that I'm not some pushover!

Wait...oh no...I'm feeling a little out of breath...
Why is everyone passing me?
Last place again...
I can feel the heat of my tears rolling down my face...
Once again darkness and defeat prevail...

This was the last time I cried about losing a race. It was also one of the last times I actually lost a neighborhood race. Everything changed for me one hot summer day. It changed because of one person. His name was John Gregory.

John was one of the foster kids my mom had taken in after his mother had died. He and his brother, Raleigh, were spitfire and hell on wheels, but they were no match for Big Ma. Most of the time, they walked lightly around her, but they ruled most of the other foster kids that lived with us. John was about 16 years old and Raleigh was around 14.

John could have easily joined in with everyone else that picked on me, but he didn't. He was not one to "go with the crowd"; in fact, he was just the opposite. He was definitely a leader and not a follower. Some might actually have called him a bully because of his impulsive and aggressive demeanor. Many of the neighborhood kids feared him. Luckily for me, he decided to take me under his wing.

On this day, he sat quietly on the side of the trailer and watched me lose that race. I guess he could see the hurt and defeat in my eyes because I watched as he strolled over to me, and in a commanding voice, told me to wipe my tears and follow him to the top of a steep hill. I immediately wiped my tears away and obediently followed him up the hill. Once on top, he suddenly grabbed my hand and we both began to run down the hill as fast as we could go. About halfway down the hill, he said, "I'm gonna let you go now, but you keep running."

It was going to be up to me if I was going to be able to keep my balance and speed or if I was going to fall flat on my face. I was absolutely terrified, but I was also tired of failing. As he let go of my hand, it felt as if everything around me was moving in slow motion. My feet were touching the ground, but it felt like I was running on air. In that moment, I was like the Roadrunner and my problems were like Wile E. Coyote. No matter how hard they tried, they couldn't catch me. It was the most exhilarating feeling I had ever had. I matched John stride for stride and we reached the bottom of the hill, neck and neck.

When we finished, he looked me in the eye and said, "Don't ever stop running."

My confidence level soared after that; I began to win races in the neighborhood. I actually looked forward to being outside and showing off my running skills. I finally had gained back some of the confidence and pride that had been stripped away from me. And I owed it all to the one person who finally showed me that he cared. Like most of the other foster kids, though, I knew John wouldn't be there for long; so I decided I would learn as much as I could from him.

Cordell Farley

Chapter 6 ~ Don't Stop Running

Fall 1981

One evening, John came into the house and told me to come outside with him to play football. Since it was just the two of us, I assumed we were going to just toss the ball back and forth. Boy, was I wrong!!! He immediately told me to go to the other end of the field. He told me that he was going to throw the ball to me and that I would have to get past him in order to score a touchdown. Sounded easy enough, right?

The first time he threw me the ball, I ran it all the way down the field and scored a touchdown. In fact, I ran it back for a touchdown two more times right after the first without being touched. It felt so good. I was outrunning the dude who had taught me to run! I thought that he had started getting tired because he told me that once I scored another touchdown, we would head into the house for the night. *This is going to be a piece of cake*, I thought to myself. My chest was poked out like a peacock; I was ready to score this last touchdown and go in for dinner.

BOOM!!! That was the noise I heard as I looked around and realized I was laid out on the ground. What had just happened? I remembered the ball touching my hand, but then, suddenly, I was laid out on the ground. John had blindsided me and hit me with a real football maneuver. He looked down at me and asked me if I was tough enough now to get past him and score a touchdown. I tried and tried for about an hour to score another touchdown. I tried everything – over him, under him, around him - and each time he knocked me squarely to the ground.

I became enraged. Tears and sweat flowed down my face as I kept pushing. This only seemed to get him more excited as the hits became harder and harder. By now, it was completely dark outside and I was ready to go in, but I knew he wouldn't let me until I scored again. I could never get past him going toe-to-toe because he was twice my size, so I hatched a plan. I would have to use my wits against his brute.

I would use the darkness to my advantage: everyone else in my life seemed to. John hiked the ball to me and I ran left, but because it was pitch black out there, he didn't see me fake out and quickly change direction to the right. SCORE!!!!

He looked me straight in the eyes and told me what a good job I had done. No one had ever genuinely praised me before and it felt good. He also told me that he felt I was ready to join a real team. I beamed at the possibility of playing organized sports. I wanted to get away from the madness at home and this was the perfect way to do it, even if it was for only a few times a week. Soon after, I signed up for my first recreational football team.

I really don't know who paid my sign-up fee; I was just excited to be a part of a team, and although I was one of the youngest, I didn't care because it felt good to be a part of something special. It was also the very first year that they integrated the black and the white teams in the recreational league. Although it was the early 1980s, our small town was still playing catch up in regards to integrating sports. My very first coaches were TC Peebles and Ronnie Roark. Those of us (black and white) under their tutelage could see and feel their passion for sports because it emanated through their attitudes and work ethic.

Chapter 7 ~ Safe Zone

Fall 1982 – Age 9

I was so excited when I finally did begin to go to football practice at the local VFW/community center. My football practices became my "safe spot." I knew that it was the one place where I didn't have to watch my back. It was also the one place where I felt like I belonged. The coaches, although they were firm, genuinely seemed to care about my well-being. It was a whole new world for me - such a contrast to everything I had ever known.

Time seemed to fly when I stepped out onto the football field. I could run and run for hours and not have to think about anything. There didn't seem to be enough practices and games to fill my time. I wanted and needed more of this euphoric feeling. So when football season ended, I eagerly signed up for Little League Baseball. I didn't know much about it, but one thing was for sure. It would get me out of the house. That, alone, was enough for me.

I had a deep desire to fill the empty void within my soul and, for now, being a part of baseball and football teams was just what I needed. At that time, I really couldn't make sense of the empty feeling I felt. Surprisingly, I feel that it had little to do with the sexual abuse from my foster sisters or the verbal abuse from Big Ma. I think it had more to do with feeling no real connection with my family. I would see them show affection towards Mary and my nieces, but when it came to me, it was almost nonexistent.

Most of the foster kids that came to stay with us were still connected with someone from their biological family in some shape or form. Sometimes, they even came in with a sibling or siblings. I could see the connection between them. I, on the other hand, didn't feel connected to anyone. There was just a sense of emptiness that was constantly looming over me. Everyone in my family was so distant and dismissive of me that it felt like I was one of the foster kids that came in and out of the house.

Why couldn't I connect to them the way they connected with each other? Why didn't they show me the same compassion and tolerance that they displayed towards one another? Why did I not have the freedom to express myself? Why didn't I feel comfortable? Why did I get in trouble when I displayed any emotions? Why was I called a dummy constantly and the threat of being sent to a mental institution held over my head? Why? Why? Why?

I had so many questions and no answers. What did all of this mean?

Chapter 8 ~ Homerun!

"Mann, go look under the bed and get my black shoes."

Oh gosh, which pair is it? There's about five black pairs of shoes under here…I won't dare ask her…I'll just pick a pair…please, God, let these be the ones she wants…Please let me get it right…

Here you go, Big Ma…Are these the ones you wanted?

"No, you dumb-a**! It's the other black ones!"

CRACK!

That was the sound of the ashtray whizzing past my head and hitting the wall in the family room of our trailer. Big Ma had a ritual of getting me to fetch her black shoes from under the bed. The problem for me, though, was that most of her shoes were black and she expected me to know which pair she wanted. She didn't say "the black ones with the buckle" or the "black ones with the strings" – only "the black ones." It was if she expected me to read her mind and I had better not dare ask for clarification on the pair she wanted. My best bet would be to become a psychic at that moment and hope and pray I got it right. But most of the time, I was wrong.

As usual, on this particular Saturday morning, I had gotten it wrong. She cussed me so bad that I ran to my secret place and prayed my sacred prayer; however, I quickly gathered myself when I realized it was game day for my baseball team. I knew that for a few hours I would get to have some sense of normalcy.

I didn't want to wait to experience that feeling, so I took off for the field. I knew that my game wasn't scheduled until later that evening, but it didn't matter. I had to get out of there. At 8 years old, I walked all by myself to the baseball field that was at least 3 miles from my house. The sun was beating down on my head, but I didn't care. I just knew I had to be there. It didn't matter that the gate was locked and would remain that way for at least another four hours. I kind of liked it that way because I immediately began to feel a sense of peace. It was a quiet time that I welcomed.

When the coaches and my teammates finally began to arrive, I fell right into place as if nothing had happened. Besides, I didn't want them to know anything was wrong. I had learned how to hide my feelings and my emotions, and had become an expert on numbing my pain. This day would be no different.

The game started out pretty routine and uneventful. We were playing the best team in our league and our hopes of possibly pulling out an upset were quickly fading as the game progressed. The stands were filled with lots of supportive white parents from both teams and the rest of the "fans" were all the black neighborhood kids and adults who didn't have anything else to do.

During the bottom of the sixth inning (we played a total of seven), someone threw a wild pitch and we scored. That locked up the game; the score was now tied. Somehow we kept them from scoring at the top of the seventh. If we could get one score at the bottom of this inning, we would win the game. The first two batters quickly struck out and suddenly, as I looked around, I realized I was next to bat. I was so nervous that I started shaking. Everyone was counting on me to end this game right now with a score. I couldn't let them down.

As the pitcher slung the ball toward me, there was a desperation that arose inside of me that wouldn't allow me to miss contact with that ball. I gritted my teeth, tightened my gut and smacked the ball clear across the left field fence. HOMERUN!!!

I had just hit my first homerun AND we won the game! The feeling was exhilarating! I would have done anything to be able to take that moment and bottle it up for safekeeping, but I knew that was impossible. So, I just celebrated for as long as I could with my coaches and teammates. It felt so good to finally be acknowledged and congratulated for doing something good.

I was on such a high after the game that I had forgotten what had happened earlier that morning with Big Ma. All I wanted to do was tell them about the game in the hopes that they would want to celebrate the moment with me, too. As I stood on the steps preparing to go into the house, I thought to myself, *Maybe they'll notice my dirty uniform when I walk in and ask me about my game.* My heart jumped at the thought that I would be able to share this feeling and excitement with them.

As I walked in, Granddaddy was sitting quietly in his usual spot in the living room watching something on the TV. He turned his head slightly and looked over his glasses to see who had just come in. When he realized it was me, he just turned his head back to the TV without so much as a grunt of acknowledgment. I decided to walk across the living room in front of him in the hopes that he would notice all the dirt and grass stains on my uniform. But he didn't even bother to glance up at me. I wanted so badly to share the experience of my first homerun with him, but I could see in his eyes that he was totally disinterested and had no desire to have any kind of conversation with me. I turned away and went to the kitchen to eat supper as tears streamed down my tired and dirty face. I didn't even bother to look for Big Ma for support as I couldn't take another rejection at that moment.

After supper, I quietly slipped away and went outside to my secret hiding place out in the empty field for the second time that day. With my heart now aching, I slowly repeated my mantra, "This too shall pass. This too shall pass."

Over the next couple of years outside of school, my time consisted of playing my heart out in whatever sport I could sign up for in an attempt to escape the pain and anguish I endured having to be at home. I racked up trophy after trophy for MVP in every sport with the recreation league, but I was no one's MVP at home. My Uncle Willy was no longer around. My protector, John had come of age and left, and my brother and best friend Randy had left not too long after John. Although there were still people in the house, I was alone - again.

Cordell Farley

Chapter 9 ~ Baby Michael

Winter 1983

By the time I was about to turn 11years old, the influx of foster kids had slowed down tremendously, but the house was still full. We also still had approximately 11 mentally disabled elderly people that lived with us – 2 in the house and the other 7 in the "small cabinets or shacks" on the property. There were a couple of foster kids left, although I don't recall exactly how many. What I do know is that all three of the girls that had violated me were gone. By this time, my nieces had also moved out and were married with children. My niece, Linda, however, had recently moved back in with her baby girl, LaJuya (named after Big Ma). Mary, of course, was also still there.

The process of taking care of elderly people was an intense one, especially the ones with severe mental illnesses, and now that I had gotten older, many of the duties had become my responsibility. I would get up every morning at 5am and begin my daily ritual. While everyone else was asleep, my first chore was to cook a full breakfast for the elderly residents. This usually consisted of bacon, eggs, fried potatoes and toast or biscuits. After cooking it all, I would make individual plates and cover them in aluminum foil. It took about three trips in the below freezing temperatures to get all of the plates delivered to each resident. Because many of them were mentally ill, I never really knew what to expect when I delivered their breakfast. Sometimes things flowed without incident, but other times, it was pure madness.

There was one particular resident named Esther who loved to water her flowers outside of her shack. Unfortunately for me, she also seemed to like hosing me down when I would try to deliver her food to her. Other times, food was thrown back at me or I'd just get cussed out to the high heavens. It was anyone's guess on any given day as to what would happen.

After completing that task (if that was what you could call it), my next job was to feed all of the dogs we had out in the backyard. At any given time, we would usually own several mutts. By the time I would finish feeding the dogs, most of the residents would be finished with their breakfast, so I would go back to collect all of their dirty and, oftentimes, broken breakfast dishes. My last and final task before getting dressed for school was the one I dreaded the most – cleaning up the horrendous mess that I made each morning cooking breakfast. I knew better than to walk out of the door without cleaning every last dish. But I also knew I'd better not miss the bus, so it was always a mad dash to get dressed and get out to the bus stop by 7:30 each morning. Some days that meant not brushing my teeth or washing my face. I would rather have funky breath and a dirty face than to feel the wrath of Big Ma for missing the bus.

This was life day in and day out until one morning a lady from Social Services knocked on the door. I thought she was there to question why an 11-year-old was taking care of a bunch of old, crazy people. No way – life just didn't play out that way back then, well at least not for me anyway.

When she stepped in the door, she was holding something in her hand. As I passed her to head out the door for school, I noticed that the "something" was a newborn baby. We never got babies from Social Services, so it was quite a surprise and kind of exciting. I couldn't wait to get back home from school that day – this was definitely a first.

When I got home that evening, I ran into the house in anticipation of being able to see and hold the baby. For some strange reason, Big Ma was totally open to this. As I held him and he looked up at me cooing, a

31

warm feeling came across me that I had never felt before. I don't know how to describe it, but it just felt right. I knew right then that I would do everything in my power to make sure no one did any harm to him. I was going to be his protector and his caretaker, and Big Ma actually allowed me to do just that.

It was like he was my little baby boy. I fed him, I got him to sleep and I even changed his dirty diapers. I didn't mind, though, because I had a connection with him that I hadn't had with anyone else in my family. Doing my daily chores didn't seem as bad anymore because I knew when I woke up in the mornings, he'd be right there beside me on my mat on the floor. Suddenly, I didn't mind coming home from school in the evenings after practice. I knew that Baby Michael would be there waiting for me.

One morning as I was waking up to do my chores, I heard Big Ma moving around in her room. That was pretty strange because she never got up that early. Then there was a knock on the door, which was even stranger. As I peeked around the corner, I saw Big Ma opening the door for the same social worker that had just been there six months ago to deliver Baby Michael. Her next movement was toward me and it shook me to the core. Without saying a word, Big Ma scooped up Baby Michael from the floor and handed him back over to the lady standing at the door. Within a flash, he was gone.

My whole world crumbled yet again. It had felt so good to take care of someone who loved me back and to feel a connection with someone, but just like that, it was all taken away. I had nothing left but the empty and lonely feeling that I had been able to escape from for that short six months. I wanted so badly to be able to feel that warmth again, and the only other thing that had ever given me something close to it was sports. From that point forward, I completely engrossed myself into playing every sport that I could, and in the country, that meant baseball, basketball and football.

Chapter 10 ~ The Strip Down

Summer 1984

The one thing I did enjoy was taking family trips to D.C. during the summer. Big Ma's sister lived there. We would pack our bags, load up the family van and hit I-95 North to D.C. We always planned to stay for the whole weekend, but it never seemed to turn out that way. When we would arrive, everyone would be excited to see each other and everything would be great. That is, until Big Ma and my aunt would start in on each other. I can't even remember what would set them off, but before we could even get a chance to get comfortable, Big Ma would be yelling for everybody to get back in the van. They loved each other, but they just couldn't get along for more than 5 minutes.

I personally looked forward to these trips because it was an opportunity to get away from all the madness at home. The unfortunate part, though, is that I wouldn't get to enjoy it very long. But lucky for me (or so I thought), Big Ma decided to let me stay for a whole week one summer. I was finally going to get the chance to hang out with my cousins and experience a totally different environment. It would also give me the rare opportunity to interact with my two uncles – Rudolph and Rudy. They always treated me like I belonged and that feeling did not come often for me. I was definitely going to make the best of this trip.

My week got off to a really good start. I had been practicing my basketball skills in the backyard at home and I was ready to show off my skills to my two cousins. They must have thought I was pretty good too because they offered to take me to the local basketball courts to play with some of their friends. Their friends were a little bit older, but it didn't matter. According to my cousins, they were going to let the "country boy" show the "city boys" some moves. And that's exactly what I did! We won almost every game. It was the best feeling in the world! The "country boy" had whooped up on the "city boys" like they had *stole* something!

After the last game was played, I headed to one end of the court to drink some water out of the container that my aunt had so thoughtfully sent with me. I was definitely not used to this kind of royal treatment. I was so lost in my own thoughts that I didn't notice when everyone began to huddle up on the other end of the court. I also failed to notice (until it was way too late) that they all had started heading in my direction at a pretty fast pace. Before I knew it, they had circled me.

I didn't know what to do except look for my cousin Tyrone. I knew he would save me. Imagine my surprise when I finally laid eyes on him and realized he had joined in with the rest of them. Suddenly, all of them converged on me at one time. Once again, I was helpless with no one to turn to. They stripped almost every piece of clothing off of my scrawny little body and tossed them to the ground. I felt completely humiliated and defeated. In the end, I guess they really showed me just what "city boys" were really made of.

Although they may have gotten away with it, I wasn't going to let my cousin Tyrone off the hook so easily. I ran all the way back to my aunt's house practically naked with my ripped clothes in one hand and my privates covered with the other hand. I was finally going to stand up for myself and tell what had been done to me if only for this one time.

I blurted out as fast and as detailed as I could what had happened to me at the park and how Tyrone had been a part of the melee. My aunt looked at me with what I thought was sympathetic eyes. Yes! It was okay to tell an adult when someone had violated me. But that thought quickly disappeared as soon as she opened her mouth. "Toughen up, boy!" she exclaimed and then walked away as if I wasn't standing there in front of her almost naked as a jaybird. I was crushed.

Later that day, my aunt was sitting on her porch talking to one of her neighbors and, unbeknownst to her, I happened to be standing by the door listening. She was busy telling her neighbor what had happened earlier at the basketball courts when she said something that was rather strange to me. Her neighbor asked who I was and she said, "Oh yeah! My sister is taking care of him."

I really didn't understand what she meant and I didn't dare ask her. But why didn't she just say, "That's my nephew"? She could have even said, "That's my sister's son." Her words gave me a sick feeling in my stomach, but I just shook it off. It didn't mean anything, did it?

I didn't want to ruin the rest of my trip since I knew it wasn't going to last much longer, so I decided that I wouldn't be mad at my cousin anymore. The next day, they asked if I wanted to go outside and play with a couple of their friends. I agreed – no hard feelings, right? Then from out of nowhere, that same cousin told one of his friends to fight me. What was it with these people? Obviously, I didn't want to fight my cousin's friend, but I wasn't going to have much of a choice in this situation either.

The kid walked right over to me and started pushing and shoving me. I tried to fight back, but I was no match for this kid who was much older than me. He continued to pummel me until my cousin finally stopped him. This whole scene of my so called life had gotten old – all of it: the physical abuse, the sexual abuse from the years before, and, most importantly, the mental and emotional abuse. There was no place for me to escape to for peace of mind. I just wanted to be a normal kid. Was that too much to ask for?

Chapter 11 ~ He Ain't No Son of Mine

By the time I reached middle school, I was a standout athlete in every sport I played, which I made sure was year round. I played football, basketball and baseball. I liked football, I liked baseball, but basketball was my passion. I just knew I was "the man" in basketball until I met up with my fellow classmate, Mark Hazelwood, on the middle school gym court during the first week of school. That day, we played one-on-one and he completely dominated me.

What's funny is that it really wasn't his skills on the court, but more so his demeanor and attitude. Although we were the same age, his presence was strong and overbearing. It was like the "stage" or court was suddenly too big for me and he had completely absorbed it. This was another defining moment for me because although I had the skills to play any sport, I really didn't have the follow-through yet to dominate and win. I walked off of the court that day wondering how he beat me, but deep down inside, I knew the answer. He was just mentally tougher and I knew this was something I would have to work on if I wanted to get better.

By the time middle school basketball season started, I was still thinking about that day on the court with Mark. I tried to ascertain how I could translate the energy he had into my own. It finally clicked one night while playing one of our biggest rivals. As I was defending the guy heading down the court to shoot the ball, he aggressively elbowed me in the jaw as he went for the layup. An offensive foul was called and we got the ball back with three seconds to go in the half. Without hesitation, I took one step from the free throw line and just hurled the ball into the air. In the past, I would have just held the ball and let the time run out to the half, but in that moment, I wanted to do something out of my character and see where it would lead. SCORE!! I banked the shot and the crowd went wild. I was in complete shock, but at the same time, I felt something different: follow-through, mental toughness and pure dominance! These were things I knew I had needed, but had never really experienced or acquired until that moment.

Suddenly, I wanted to show off this newfound confidence to my family. I really don't know why – maybe for validation or maybe just to try and fit in. My opportunity came one particular evening as I was walking along with my nephew who happened to be about 5 years older than me and was about to start his senior year of high school in the fall. We ran up on a couple of guys who were about his age starting a pickup basketball game. He stopped to join in; however, they didn't even give me a second look. I was only 13 at the time, so I sat on the sidelines and watched, hungry to be a part of the game.

My chance finally came, though, when one of the guys got hurt during the game and my nephew's team needed a replacement. He reluctantly looked over at me and asked if I wanted to play. My immediate response was "yes" and his immediate look was "you better not ****this up!" Not only did I not mess up, but I held my own against all of the older and much more experienced players. More importantly, unlike the D.C. incident awhile back, there was no strip down after the game. Only congratulatory high fives.

My nephew was so psyched about how well I had played that he decided to walk me home so that he could tell my dad. We ran into the kitchen where Granddaddy was cooking supper. My nephew was very animated about the details of the game as I sat quietly and watched for the slightest indication from Granddaddy that he actually gave a damn. He must have sensed Granddaddy's disinterest and told him that he should be proud because one day his son was going to be a professional athlete. Granddaddy soaked in the information and hesitated about 3 seconds. Without even looking up from what he was doing, he nonchalantly replied, "That ain't my damn son!"

I didn't know what Granddaddy meant by that comment, but it cut deep. Why would he say I wasn't his son? Had I done something for him to disown me? It just didn't make sense to me. But it did make me flashback to a conversation one of my neighborhood friends and I had a couple of years back while riding bikes.

As we were riding past my house, out of the blue, he said, "You know them people you staying with ain't your real mom and dad, right?" At the time, I had totally dismissed what he had said. He was known as a big mouth and often didn't know what he was talking about. So this is the same attitude I decided to take about what my dad had just said – I tried to dismiss it. I turned and walked back outside deep in thought about what Granddaddy had just said. My nephew interrupted my thoughts. "Don't worry about it, Mann. You gone be alright," and then we walked away.

As I processed all that had just happened, I began shooting hoops in the side yard. I tried to ascertain what my nephew had said to Granddaddy while he was in the house: "he's going to be a professional athlete one day." The more I processed all that had been said, the harder I pushed myself with each shot to the net. It was almost like I had an epiphany that night: if he wasn't going to treat me like his son, then I wasn't going to try anymore to "fit in" like his son. Every time the ball fell in the net, I began to feel more and more confident about being able to control something in my life. Then, I realized that I couldn't control how they felt about me, but I could control the effort I was going to put in to make sure one day I would be able to remove myself from that house.

Sports was going to do that for me. I knew right then and there that I wanted to become a professional athlete. My nephew had apparently seen something in me that I was now fully aware of, too. I had watched professional basketball and football players on TV countless times, and they seemed to have it all and to be in control of their own destinies. I was determined that, one day, I would do the same.

Chapter 12 ~ The Academic Underachiever

Although I had found this new level of confidence on the court, it definitely didn't translate to home or my academics. The negative energy at home had become much more intense and I wanted no part of it. Granddaddy had been in a really serious car accident. He didn't get hurt, but I the other parties involved were injured and he was found to be at fault. I never really knew all of the details, but I did know that it must have been really bad because not only did they come after his insurance, they also legally pursued him as an individual. Most of his paycheck from the factory was used to pay, what I presume, were the victims of the accident.

Big Ma made it no secret about how disgusted she was with him and it also didn't help that most of her income had dried up, too. For years, she had relied on her income from Social Services for taking in foster kids and elderly people, and now most of it was gone. They say "more money, more problems," but I can attest to the fact that "no money" was much worse. Big Ma was more irritable those days than in years past. But who could blame her? The only problem was that I still took the brunt of most of that anger. I tried my best to stay under the radar when I was at home, but most of the time, it didn't work.

I did do a better job at staying under the radar at school, though, much to my detriment. Although, as I have said, I was pretty aggressive on the field and on the court, I was the opposite when it came to my academics. Because no one had ever taken an interest in how I did at school, I had a lackadaisical attitude about it. Consequently, I was placed in all lower level classes, or "slow classes" as my classmates referred to them, during my first year of middle school. I would often finish my work within a minute. Spelling words would be something like months of the year, days of the week, or even colors like red and green. Easy stuff. Still, no one noticed that I was more than capable of doing the work.

For Math, I didn't switch classes like most of the other students. Instead, I sat in the same classroom doing simple division, multiplication, addition and subtraction. I knew that some of the kids in the class really needed the help and *really* needed to be in there; I just didn't think I was one of them. It was a shameful situation, or at least I should have been ashamed, but I didn't allow myself to feel this way. I wanted to speak up, but I knew there was no one who would have my back. What did I know? Big Ma had always told me that I was dumb, so I must have belonged in there, I told myself. I went through my entire seventh grade year in that same classroom and learned nothing. I just numbed myself and pushed through.

This changed in the 8th grade. One teacher finally saw something different in me; her name was Ms. Brodie, my 8th grade teacher. I was placed in her classroom for all of the core classes back then: English, Math, Social Studies and Science. It was like that with the "slow" classes." You had one teacher for all of your main subjects. It was embarrassing to stay in one class for most of the day when all of my friends were switching classes for every period, but I felt then that I didn't have a voice to change it.

Ms. Brodie soon became that voice for me, though. One day after class, she pulled me to the side and told me that I didn't belong in her class. She had noticed how fast I finished all of the lessons and that they were always correct. I had never asked for help on any of her assignments and never struggled with any of her tests. This was definitely not the case for the other students in this class; most of the work she gave was truly a challenge for them. She told me that she was going to do everything in her power to see to it that I was placed in

41

the appropriate classes. Words cannot describe how happy I was that someone had finally realized that I was a bright kid on and off the field. All I had needed was a push in the right direction.

Chapter 13 ~ The Galax Trip: The Victory That Never Happened

Summer 1987

Mrs. Brodie followed through on her promise and I was taken out of her class and placed in the appropriate classes. It did wonders for my confidence to finally be able to switch classes for each period. There was no greater feeling each day to have work placed in front of me that was an actual challenge. It felt as if I was finally getting validation that I wasn't that dumb, stupid kid I had been repeatedly told I was. Sadly, Big Ma and Granddaddy didn't even know I was switched into more challenging classes – or if they did know, they never discussed it with me. As a matter of fact, we never "discussed" anything. She barked orders and I complied. It was as simple as that.

The confidence I had gained in school during my eighth grade year translated over to baseball that summer as we began the season for the recreation league. Although basketball and football were my first loves, I also began to make bigger strides on the baseball field. As a matter of fact, our recreational league team did so well that season that we made it to our first state tournament. I was so excited because I had never been away from home except for the trips to D.C.

For the tournament, we were going to be staying away from home for an entire week in the small mountain town of Galax, Virginia, which was about four hours away from home and near the border of Tennessee. I could barely contain myself – a whole week away from home with people who actually liked and cared about me. It just didn't get any better!

As a team, we had developed a camaraderie that I cannot put into words even today. Coach Kevin Miller was our head coach and, in some ways, he reminded me of Big Ma because of his straightforward and sometimes brutal approach. He demanded perfection, and when it didn't look as though we were putting forth all our effort, we would catch hell. Although he was pretty harsh on us, Coach Miller also showed us that he cared and that went a long way with me in particular, especially since I hadn't experienced someone yelling at me one moment and encouraging me in the next - not since my days with John, that is. His persistence and aggressiveness was what had gotten us that far.

That entire week of the tournament was like a dream come true. We were the only undefeated team and we had made it to the final game. Now all we had to do was to win the last game and bring home the trophy. It should have been simple, but nothing in my life was ever "simple." I had already learned that when life is going smooth, a curve ball quickly turned it upside down.

Well, our curve ball came in the form of our starting pitcher refusing to take the field on what should have been the championship game on the last night of our stay. We only needed to win the first game of the series and it would be over. We would be heading to Florida to the Dixie Youth World Series to represent Virginia. It was going to be a cinch, right? We had played exceptionally well all week long and hadn't lost a game. So it was truly a surprise to all of us what was happening. We couldn't believe that he was suddenly just refusing to play!

When we arrived at the field, he went straight into the stands and took a seat. He was upset and completely defeated. It turns out that he had found out the night before that a girl he liked had been messing around with one of our teammates. At our age, I guess that was supposed to be the end of the world, but I didn't get it. We were a team and teams didn't let each other down. But he didn't care about any of that at that moment. He only cared about his feelings. So he sat the game out and we lost.

I was completely devastated as was the rest of our team. We knew we were the best team and to lose because one person had put his own selfishness ahead of the team was ridiculous. With that one selfish act, he destroyed the entire chemistry of the team. Luckily for us, because, again, we were the only undefeated team at the tournament, the other team would have to beat us twice in order to claim the victory. This also meant that if we won this second match-up, we could still go home as the champs and head to Florida.

After seeing us lose a close first game, our pitcher suddenly decided he wanted to play. He probably realized that it was going to be a long ride home for him and he'd better do something to try and fix what he had so badly screwed up. We didn't care, though. He had given up on us at the most crucial point when we needed him and we weren't interested in him rejoining the team.

Although we gave a valiant effort in the second game, we ultimately lost that one, too. Everyone felt so much hurt and anger – feelings I knew all too well. The difference for me, though, was that for the first time in my life, I wasn't going through these emotions and feelings alone. Everybody totally supported each other and that feeling was indescribable. I had been through good times with my team, but experiencing that moment of hurt with them gave me a glimpse into how families really should be there for each other. I had seen it in my house, but I had just never felt it. I knew that in order for me to continue to have this feeling of connection, I would have to keep myself connected to a team.

Chapter 14 ~ Show Me the Money

Summer 1988

The following year, my teammates and I made it back to the state tournament, and this time, we won! Our next stop was the Pony League World Series in the sunshine state of Florida. Our team would be representing the state of Virginia. This was a pretty big deal and I was excited to share the news with Big Ma and Granddaddy. However, it was no surprise that they both seemed to be pretty indifferent when I made the "big" announcement that I'd be going all the way to Florida to play in the World Series. Granddaddy just stared at me with a blank look and Big Ma just said okay. She wasn't so "indifferent," though, when the next words came out of my mouth: I would need at least $100 for food on the trip.

The team had raised enough money to take care of all of the other expenses, but they had left it to the parents to cover the expense of food. Without a second thought, Big Ma told me to "get the hell out of my face" and then walked away. I didn't get a response at all from Granddaddy, which automatically meant no. There was no way I was going to miss this trip, but I knew I couldn't go to Florida broke.

I moped around the house for days racking my brain on how to get the money. Big Ma must have felt sorry for me because on the night before we left, she begrudgingly gave me three wrinkled $5 dollar bills and told me that I was going to have to make it work. How was I going to eat three meals a day for 6 days on $15? As soon as I stepped on the bus the next morning, I had my answer - a bunch of my teammates were playing cards.

Now if I hadn't learned anything else from Big Ma up to this point, I had learned how to play cards. She was "the" card lady in Blackstone. Every weekend, she held card games that literally lasted throughout the entire weekend. People didn't even go home. They would come in on Fridays with a pocket full of cash from their freshly cashed paychecks and would stay at the table until either they were completely broke or they hit it big. When it was all said and done, it really didn't matter to Big Ma who had won or lost because she always got a cut out of every game. That was the "house rule." She provided the space, food and liquor (usually of the bootleg persuasion) and, in return, she got a cut. It was always a win-win situation for her.

On this particular morning, I was going to make it a win-win for me. Throughout the years, I had quietly sat in the shadows at Big Ma's card games and learned every trick of the game. Now, it was time to use them. I was in survival mode. My teammates didn't know what had hit 'em when they dealt me in. I had always been so quiet that I'm sure they thought playing with me would be like taking candy from a baby. They were in for a rude awakening. The shy and quiet boy hustled every one of them. By the time we got to Florida, I had won $95. I now had $110 for the week. Give a boy $15 and he'll eat for a day; teach him how to play cards, and he'll eat for at least 6 days!

Although we didn't win the World Series, I left with something much more profound. Throughout the week, we had the opportunity to listen to several different speakers, but there was one that stood out to me the most. He was a real major league baseball scout. He told us that there was a lot of talent in baseball, but you had to look like a pro player in order to be noticed out of the crowd. He made it seem so plain and simple. I didn't truly understand the meaning of it at the time, but I knew that what he said spoke to something in my core being. I knew that although I was talented and I now had the mental toughness it took to excel in any sport, I was still lacking something. What did "look like a pro player" really mean and how would I acquire this look? I was about to head into high school and I knew that this attitude would somehow play into how well or poorly I did at this next level.

As he spoke, I recalled a vivid memory I had about our school district's high school football team. For the first time ever in the history of our school district, the football team had made it to the state championship. The image of those players climbing onto the bus that brisk fall morning with serious expressions on their faces as if they were heading into battle burned clearly in my mind. I also remembered the feeling I had as my two best friends and I watched their bus pull away. Then, it clicked. They had set the standard, and I knew that what the scout was talking about at that moment was somehow tied to the burning feeling I felt as I remembered the look on the faces of those football players. I was going into battle.

Chapter 15 ~ Say "Cheese!"

As I entered into my freshman year of high school, there was an interesting dynamic going on in my household. Big Ma couldn't stand Granddaddy, he steered clear of her, they both doted on my sister Mary and they all seemed to have a clear disdain for me. Linda had moved out, but her daughter, LaJuya (or Juicy as we called her), had stayed. Juicy was about 8 years old and I had become like a big brother to her, so she was the only one in the house that really didn't fit into the dynamic of the negative energy that circulated between me and the rest of the members of my household.

Miraculously, I had also finally "earned" my own bedroom since all of the elderly people and foster kids were now gone. I was becoming an outstanding athlete and was also beginning to become more comfortable with myself. I no longer walked around the house with my head down, trying to stay out of everyone's way. I don't think that sat too well with anyone in my house, however. It was as if they were irritated by the fact that I was doing so well in sports and that I was no longer the shy, timid kid trying to stay under the radar. And although their words were few, their actions spoke volumes to me.

No one ever showed up to any of my games nor did they ever bother to ask how I did or just a quick, "Did you win?" There were times when I would look into the stands or bleachers to see if anybody had showed up to see me play, even though I already knew that they hadn't. It was moments like these when I would lose focus and ask myself what it was all for - why was I even bothering to do it? Thankfully, those moments were rare.

Although they never showed up to any games, I always knew they were at least thinking of me. When I would get home from football practice or a game, there would be a kitchen full of dishes waiting just for me. They knew I would be exhausted by the time I got home, especially on a game night, but that didn't matter. I had better have those dishes washed before I went to bed or all hell would break loose the next morning.

I decided to try my luck one night because I was just so dog-tired that I could only make it into the house and to my bed. I was suddenly awakened in the middle of the night by ice cold water splashing all over my face and body. Big Ma had come in late from a card game and discovered a kitchen full of dirty dishes. She was livid and screamed, "Get your **damn a** up and wash those dishes!" I immediately jumped up and flew past her before she could catch me with a right hook. From that moment on, I never neglected my duty of washing those dishes after a game. It didn't matter how tired I was.

At school, no one knew of the excruciating pain I was enduring at home on a daily basis. I had become the master of masking my true feelings. I walked around school with a smile plastered on my face. No matter how I was feeling, I just smiled through it. I think everybody at school either thought I was the happiest dude in the world or I was just a goofball. As a matter of fact, in middle school, Coach Miller and my teammates called me "Cheese" because they said I always looked like I was getting ready for the camera. By the time I had reached my freshman year in high school, everyone was calling me "Cheese." Although it was okay for Coach Miller and my teammates to call me that, because they knew me and cared about me, it wasn't a pleasant feeling to hear other people call me that. But I simply brushed it off like I did everything else in my life. Sadly, it was beginning to get harder and harder to brush things off.

During the summer before my sophomore year, I considered not even trying out for football. It was not because I didn't want to play, but something else was eating at me even more. I had grown tired of wearing the same hand-me-down clothes to school every day. Each year, I watched everybody walk into the school with their fresh new threads and it just gnawed at me that I didn't have what they had. But I knew no one would buy me new clothes, so I made the decision to look for a job instead of trying out for football. I wanted to take control of something in my life – even if it was just buying myself some new clothes.

As football tryouts began, I started putting in applications at different local stores in our town, but I wasn't getting any calls for interviews (meanwhile, three of my friends had each put in one application and had pretty much been hired on the spot). One day, there was a knock on the door and when I went to answer it, there stood Coach Dickie Ingram, one of the coaches for the varsity football team.

He said, "I understand you're not trying out for football this year. We would really like to have you out there."

This was a great feeling for me to hear someone tell me that they wanted me. At the same time, I was also tired of looking like a hobo. I explained to him that although I really wanted to try out, I needed money to buy shoes and clothes for the upcoming year. He told me that he had a friend at one of the local restaurants and he would try to get me on for the weekends so that I could still play football during the week. That was enough to sell me! I was ready to play some football.

I made the varsity team as the back-up quarterback and soon forgot all about wanting the job or the new clothes. I was on the varsity football team. How could it get any better? Well, I was about to find out soon. We had lost the first four games of the season and then the starting quarterback, without notice, decided to quit. Suddenly, I was thrust into the spotlight – I was now the starting quarterback for the varsity team who had lost the first four games of the season. I knew this was an opportunity for me to shine and I didn't want to disappoint myself or the fans who had become accustomed to an outstanding team (even though this team hadn't exactly shown that winning spirit all the fans were used to).

We ended up winning the remaining six games of the season and just missed making the playoffs. I was on cloud nine for that huge accomplishment in my life. I had made a difference and an impact – and it mattered. This energy was enough to carry me through school for the rest of the year and it generated into my other two favorite sports: basketball and baseball. I made the varsity team for both of these as well. Still no one showed up to my games but at that point it didn't really matter to me.

When my junior year rolled around, I automatically assumed that I would be the starting quarterback for the football team again. I mean why wouldn't I think that? I had helped turned what was a disappointing losing season into a winning one. I was ready to play. What I wasn't ready for was what actually happened; during tryouts, a senior who had been ineligible the year before, was selected to be the starting quarterback. I was completely baffled and totally deflated. I just stood there watching the offense run plays without me. Another guy was in my position and I didn't understand how it had happened.

At that moment, as I watched in dismay, I felt a strong hand on my shoulder and a tap on my helmet. It was Coach Billy Boswell. Coach Boswell had been my head coach for junior varsity and he was one of the assistant coaches for the varsity team. He looked me square in the eyes and said in what was always his compassionate tone towards players, "Cordell, hang in there and keep your head up. You never know when your number will be called."

He quietly walked away as I stood there, still devastated, but also appreciating the fact that he had taken the time to pull me to the side and give me a pep talk. This moment showed me that even when things weren't going my way, there was a certain way to handle it and to always be prepared for anything. I still don't know for sure if this is what happened, but I believe Coach Boswell later advocated for me to play on defense that year at the safety position. I ended up making eleven interceptions on defense. His lesson had rung true. We made it all the way to the state championship that year. It was the second time in our school's history that we had made it that far. We didn't win that final game, but the lessons I learned during that season and during that final game were much more valuable than I could have imagined and would prepare me for the storm I was about to encounter.

Chapter 16 ~ The Ugly Truth – Coming of Age

Summer 1991 – Age 18

By the time I reached the summer before my senior year, the idea of becoming a professional athlete was one that I now knew I wanted to be a reality. I knew it would be a way to get away from all of the turmoil that always seemed to engulf my life and suffocate me. Being a part of a team made me feel like I was a part of a family and it also helped me shake that suffocating feeling.

Being promiscuous also helped drown out that feeling. It was a normal thing for guys my age to be sexually active (especially the athletes), but I argue that I was a bit looser in this area than most – probably triggered by what had happened to me as a young boy with my foster sisters. I was only 12 years old the first time I "chose" to have sex. Although the girl was older than me, I didn't feel like she had violated me as my foster sisters had done in the past. After that first time, there were periods when I would just go for it as often as possible, especially when things were really bad at home. It was *my* choice and it made *me* feel good in that moment. But the feeling never lasted.

No matter how much I told myself that I didn't care how my family treated me, in reality, it just wasn't true. The same questions would flow back and forth in my head. Why was there no connection between me and them? Why were they so dismissive of me? Why hadn't I earned their love or praise? I racked my brain for the answers to these questions, but nothing made sense. I wasn't a troublemaker, I made decent grades, I was an outstanding athlete and I always obeyed them. What else could I have done to get their approval?

One day, as I sat around contemplating my life, certain moments throughout my childhood began to stand out to me. My aunt saying back in 1984: "My sister taking care of him." Granddaddy in the summer of 1986: "That boy ain't my damn son!" My big mouthed childhood friend: "You know them people ain't your real mom and dad, right?"

What did all of this mean? Was there a remote possibility that somehow I wasn't their biological child? That couldn't be! I distinctly remembered when I was little one of my foster brothers asked Big Ma if I was their "real son" and she said yes. Why would she lie about that? As I sat there, I tried to shake the rising anxiety that began to set in my soul. I couldn't shake it and I couldn't dismiss it. But it wouldn't matter for too long. It all finally came to a head one evening during that summer.

As usual, Big Ma began fussing at me about something as soon as I walked into the door - I don't even remember what it was. I just knew I had reached my breaking point. I said something to the effect that I felt like I had to work for food or work for anything I got in the house. It was the first time I had been bold enough to stand up for myself. Big Ma immediately started firing off every cuss word she could think of. I'm sure she was pretty surprised that I had talked back to her.

As she continued to rant and rave, I just walked off toward my room. I couldn't take it anymore. My sister Mary followed me down the hall in complete disbelief that I had walked away while Big Ma was still talking, but I was so angry and so tired, I really didn't care. I remember mumbling under my breath as I walked into the bathroom something to the effect of, 'I know she's not my mom anyway,' out of pure frustration. I didn't mean for anyone to hear me, but the words carried a little bit louder than I had anticipated.

My sister must have heard me because she suddenly appeared at the bathroom door - that I happened to still have open - and asked me, "What did you say?"

I looked her square in the eyes. I didn't want to repeat what I had just said, but it was too late. I needed to embrace the fear that had completely taken over me. It felt as if I was having an out of body experience as I repeated the words, "I know she's not my mom anyway." I didn't know this to be fact, but it was just a feeling that I had. I didn't know what would come after I uttered those words, but there was no turning back.

"WELL, SHE'S THE ONLY MOTHER YOU'VE EVER KNOWN!"

The words felt like a dagger that went straight into my heart. What had she just said to me? I repeated the words to myself: *She's the only mother you've ever known!* Everything started rushing to my head. Every suspicion I had recently been feeling suddenly became a heartbreaking reality. I really *wasn't* their child? How could this be? I carried their last name. As I was processing these words, Big Ma was processing *my* words, although I don't think she had heard mine clearly.

"What did he say? What did he say?" she repeatedly screamed at Mary as she headed down the hall toward us.

Not knowing what kind of firestorm she had created, Mary timidly repeated back to Big Ma what I had said. "He said you're not his real mom anyway." Her eyes darted back and forth between the both of us as the words flowed like a river out of her mouth.

All hell broke loose!! As I stood there, I attempted to process what had just happened. I didn't have long to do that, though, because as soon as I turned to look in the mirror, Big Ma's fist came crashing down on my head. She couldn't pick up stuff quick enough to hurl at me. The closest thing in her reach was a bar of soap, but she quickly put that down because I guess that wouldn't have inflicted enough damage.

As she walked out of the bathroom toward the kitchen, she shouted back at me, "You're lucky we took your black a** in! We should've let you stay with them so they could have thrown your a** in the pond or left your a** in the trashcan!!! GET THE F*** OUT OF MY HOUSE!!!!!"

All these words were being thrown at me as she turned back towards me and began hitting me with a flyswatter she had picked up on her way to the kitchen. The flyswatter was quickly bent as she swung wildly at my head and body. She finally got a hold of something heavy and hurled it toward me just as I was running out of the house. I don't even remember what it was, but I knew it was heavy enough to cause excruciating pain to my shoulder. That physical pain was nothing, though, in comparison to the pain I was feeling emotionally.

DARKNESS. No words of comfort…no check-in of my mental state. Only a physical lashing and barrage of crushing words to confirm to me that I was the product of the foster care system. Other questions then began to pop up in my head as I began to run. Why had they kept me? Why did I have their last name? What did she mean when she said they should have let me stay with "them" and let "them" throw me into the pond…or the trashcan? Who was "them"?

I ran all the way to my older sister's house about 3 miles away. I needed someone to tell me what was going on. I was pretty confident that my brother-in-law would do just that. He was a straight shooter and didn't mince words. My intent was to never return home. I wanted them to take me in, but I just needed to get some answers first. As I walked through the screen door of her house, a look of horror on my face, I blurted out, "She kicked me out and I know they are not my real parents." I didn't know how else to tell them what had just happened only a few minutes before.

My brother-in-law immediately responded as if he had been preparing for this day. He said, "Mann, it's a long story, one I don't think you really want to know. You need to go back home, finish school, leave and don't ever come back."

I was even more confused now. I began to question everything I thought to be true throughout my life. But more importantly, I did not want to go back home. I also knew I had disrespected Big Ma, so she most likely wasn't going to allow me back anyway. "Can I stay with y'all for a while until things calm down?" I pleaded.

Although I could tell he felt sorry for me, he replied, "No, you need to go back home."

I was completely devastated and alone. I had many more questions now than I had answers. My nephew was home from college for the summer and he had been in the room during my interaction with his dad. He decided to walk me back home. As we walked, he stopped and looked at me with compassion in his eyes. He said, "Mann, there are a lot of things that went on in this family that you don't want to know about and you're better off not knowing; trust me, you don't really want to know."

After he spoke those words, he walked away, leaving me to my thoughts. At that very moment, I realized that everyone in the family had known from the very beginning my true parentage except for me. I continued to walk towards Big Ma's house deep in thought. As I got closer to the house, I could hear Big Ma outside talking, but she didn't know that I was within earshot. She kept saying, "He's a good boy and he never gave me any trouble, but he can't stay here." I could hear a pain in her voice that I had never heard before, but what she was saying was even more painful to me. I walked right past her and back into the house. I couldn't even bring myself to look at her in the face.

Granddaddy, who hardly ever said anything to me, motioned for me to come out to the backyard. His first words to me were, "What are you going to do?"

I said, "I don't know, but I know I can't stay here."

He replied, "Well, you don't have anywhere else to go. You might as well just stay here and when you finish school, you can go. Later on, if you want to find your real parents, I will help you."

Everything was so surreal at that moment: real parents? What did that even mean? There couldn't be any "real" parents because if they existed and they were "real," they wouldn't have given me away to strangers. I shook my head and just kept saying, "I can't stay here."

And each time, he responded with, "You have nowhere to go. You can stay here." He finally wore me down when I realized that I truly had nowhere else to go. Again he repeated, "I will help you find your parents when you finish school."

I knew he was just trying to pacify me at that point to calm the situation, but I also knew that, in reality, I had nowhere else to go and that I would have to tough it out through my senior year. I presume he worked it out with Big Ma because she didn't object to me coming back in the house later that night. As a matter of fact, she was unusually quiet for the rest of the night. I'm guessing that she had never processed having to deal with something like this. All of the other kids that had come in and out of her home knew they didn't belong to her and their stays were always temporary. I, on the other hand, had been there for 18 years and didn't know that I didn't "technically" belong to her. As I sat in my room playing over and over in my head what had just happened, I felt as if darkness and light were in a vicious battle for my soul.

Chapter 17 ~ The Awakening

Fall 1991 – Senior Year

Suddenly, everything made sense to me, yet, at the same time, nothing made sense at all. Who was I? Where did I belong? I certainly hadn't been made to feel like I belonged to these people I had called my mom and dad all my life. If they didn't really want me, then why did they take me in? These were questions that I knew would not get answered. Everything that was said that night was left right where it was. There were no explanations nor were there any "check-ins" to see how I was feeling after finding out such devastating news. It was as if nothing had happened. The intensity of the disdain towards me seemed to subside, but the attitude of indifference remained the same. Strangely, and to my complete and utter surprise, they even bought me a car, perhaps out of guilt. I really didn't know what to make of anything. But rather than continuing to rack my brain with all of the lingering questions or allow the pain to eat away at me, I decided to do what I did best: play ball.

It was my senior year; football season was right in front of me, and I had something to prove. I had been relegated to playing safety the previous year and now it was my turn to shine at starting quarterback, the position I felt had been ripped from me my junior year. All of the excitement that everyone usually feels about their senior year and finishing school wasn't lost on me, but my energy was directed all in one place: leading my team back to the state championship and winning it this time. I was so confident that we could do it, I went to our new principal and promised her that we were going to win. My only request from her was that if we won, each of us would get state championship rings. And she agreed.

As a team, we locked in on that goal. I needed this – it was my lifeline. While most seniors were concerned about completing college applications, I was more concerned about how to lead my team to the next victory. We fought hard and we fought as one. That perseverance paid off and we found ourselves back in the state finals again. It was our destiny.

As we arrived on our home field at Golubic Stadium (better known as "The Rock") that morning to prepare for the biggest game of our lives, I could feel the excitement in the atmosphere. The stands were packed and the entire stadium was standing-room only. Before we kicked off, I looked around the field and locked eyes with the same two friends who had been with me on that cold, fall morning years ago in middle school when we watched the bus leaving to carry the varsity football team to the state championship. They had gone into battle that day and fought hard, but lost.

During my junior year, we had come close again, but left without a victory. I felt in every bone of my body that it was our turn this year and we would be victorious, and I knew the guys that surrounded me felt the exact same way. This battle was ours to win and we did just that. The final score was 28-12. It was one of the best feelings in the world to experience victory on that level. We had worked hard as a team and accomplished the ultimate goal.

After football season ended, I immediately shifted gears to playing basketball. Our basketball team had never won a state championship game and I knew we wouldn't win that year either. We had a mediocre team at best that year, but that was the sport that I had the most passion for. It was also the sport I was hoping would get me a scholarship for college. My goal after graduating was to go to North Carolina (NC) State and play basketball for them. The reality, though, was that I didn't have the grades to be accepted into NC State.

Let me back it up even a little further. I hadn't even taken the appropriate classes to be accepted. Although Ms. Brodie, my 8th grade teacher, had pushed to get me out of the slow classes in middle school, I still hadn't taken the more advanced classes in high school that I would need in order to get into a four year university. I had assumed that my guidance counselor had looked at my transcripts from middle school and had placed me in all basic level courses because those were the classes I had taken all four years in high school. They were enough to get me a high school diploma, but surely weren't enough to get me into ANY four year university, let alone a Division I school. I had only taken "general" classes and I hadn't done so hot in them. All I knew to do was the minimum to stay on sports teams and that's what I did. Unfortunately for me, what I had worked so hard for was about to slip out of my reach. I just didn't know it yet.

It started to become a reality to me, however, when basketball season ended and I hadn't received any phone calls about being recruited. I just knew that I should have received a phone call by now about either football or basketball because some of my friends were getting those phone calls. How was it that they were being recruited, but I wasn't? I had been the leader on both teams: football and basketball. It didn't occur to me that what was hindering me were my grades. As always, I moved those thoughts to the side and kept plugging along. It was almost baseball season and I thought I needed to refocus my energy there while I waited for the phone call.

Baseball season came and we definitely didn't have any hope of going to the state finals. I played centerfield and was pretty decent at it, but baseball really wasn't my thing. However, it kept me from having to be at home, so it was a win-win for everyone. One night while riding the bus from an away game, I was listening to music on my headphones, totally engrossed in the song "Poison," by BBD, when my head baseball coach, Whip Wilson, tapped me on the shoulder.

He said, "Farley, what are you going to do?"

I responded, "Um, I'm going to college."

"Have you filled out any college applications? Have you completed your financial aid package?" he asked. I was dumbfounded because the answer to both questions was no.

The following day, Coach Wilson called me into his office and told me I had two choices: Louisburg Junior College, a two year school in North Carolina that I had never heard of, or Bluefield College, a small school in the mountains of Virginia that, again, I had never heard of. After I had worked so hard on the field, these were my only two choices. I had to accept the fact that although I had worked hard on the field, I had not given the same effort in the classroom. I had always dreamed of becoming a professional athlete and I thought my first step in that plan was to be accepted into a Division I school and receive an athletic scholarship for football or basketball. How wrong was I! I had to quickly change gears and adjust my plan. I wasn't going to deviate from the ultimate goal of becoming a professional athlete, but I now knew I would have to modify how I would become one.

Coach Wilson helped me complete my application to Louisburg College and all of the other necessary paperwork. When I was accepted to Louisburg, there was no "signing day" or scholarships offers to review or accept; it was just a simple letter that came in the mail. I didn't say a word to Big Ma or Granddaddy, although there was a huge buzz around town about what I was going to do next. But whether or not they had heard anything, I didn't have a clue to because they never once spoke a word to me about it. I just knew this letter was my ticket out.

The rest of my senior year ticked by slowly. All of the sports that I played were now over and there was nothing left to do except to look forward to my graduation. I actually attended my senior prom, which I think was a shock to myself and everyone else since I really hadn't been involved in those types of extracurricular activities before. I had lived and breathed sports, but for the moment, they were over and I decided I would make the most of what time was left.

My graduation from high school was pretty uneventful. I don't even remember if Big Ma and Granddaddy showed up. I just knew I was ready to close this chapter of my life. This summer before college seemed to drag on for an eternity. I spent most of my days playing basketball at the gym at Fort Pickett, the military base that was located in our town. I knew I needed to be ready to prove my skills when I arrived on campus to try out for the basketball team. I had a one track mind: get to Louisburg, stay there for one semester long enough to play on the basketball team, and be ready to transfer to NC State or Virginia Tech the following year. It was my master plan.

Chapter 18 ~ The College Basketball Tryout

Fall 1992

In the fall of 1992, Granddaddy and one of his nephews loaded all of my things into his station wagon and dropped me off at the dorm in Louisburg, North Carolina. Before they left, Granddaddy's nephew decided to give me what he probably thought was some parting wisdom. "It's all on you now," he said, which I found quite ironic since it had been that way for me for as long as I could remember.

I brushed it off and waved goodbye to my old life. I had better things to do and I wanted to jump in head first. My first plan of action was to try out for the basketball team as a walk-on because they did not have a football program. Although basketball season didn't kick off until November, tryouts were held in September. It was my chance to shine again and I was ready for the challenge.

Each day during tryouts, we had to run a 2.7 mile hike through a hilly neighborhood in 18 minutes and I was killing it. After the run each day, we walked back to campus in a group. One particular day, another guy and I decided to take a different route and cut through a lady's yard to see if we could get back to campus a little faster because we were starving. As we were cutting through, we accidentally knocked off a small piece of board from her fence. We didn't think anything of it because it was small and we really hadn't damaged anything.

By the time we got back to campus, we were summoned to the coach's office. He told us that a man had been to his office and had informed him that he saw us trespassing and vandalizing someone's property. We tried to explain what had really happened, but it fell upon deaf ears. Coach proceeded to tell me that he had been looking forward to me being on the team, but in light of what had happened, he couldn't afford to jeopardize his program with a young man willing to indulge in risky behavior.

Me, indulge in risky behavior? I had never even been called to the principal's office in high school. I had always lived under the radar and now one split-second decision was about to crush all of my dreams. My basketball career had ended before it even got started and I had no one to blame except myself.

I had always faced rejection at home, but I had never faced rejection by a team. I had been a part of some type of sports team since I was five years old. To me, team equaled family and suddenly, I was left with no family. I became so depressed that I stopped working out, I barely attended classes and I did a lot of drinking and partying.

By the end of my first semester, I had gained 25 pounds and my GPA was 1.2. I was immediately put on academic probation and was told that if I didn't pull my GPA up to a 2.0 by the end of the second semester, I would be suspended indefinitely. That meant I would be sent packing straight back to the hell I had worked so hard to get away from. This was my wake-up call. If I wasn't sure of anything else, I was sure that I didn't want to end up back in Blackstone working a dead end job and being faced with the reality that I had failed. So, if I couldn't play sports, I needed to make the best of the situation and at least get an education.

By the end of the second semester, I managed to get a 3.7, which pulled my GPA up to a 2.45, and I was taken off of academic probation. I had never had to work so hard on my academics, but I knew everything was on the line. If I were to ever set foot back on any type of playing field, I knew I had to give the same amount of energy to my classes that I had given to sports all my life.

This was a first for me and it felt good. Although I would have to return home for the summer (I really didn't have anywhere else to go), I knew it wouldn't be for long because now I was eligible to return to school in the fall. A flicker of light....

Chapter 19 ~ Turning Point

Fall 1993

My summer at home was pretty uneventful. I spent most of it working at a lumber yard. This was even more motivation for me to figure out how I would get sports back into my life. My ultimate goal was to become a professional athlete. I just hadn't figured out yet how I would do it. In the meantime, my relationship with my family was pretty much the same. I had learned to numb myself when I was with them in order to get through. They didn't care about me and I had learned to have the same attitude towards them.

I returned to school in the fall where I was determined to focus on my academics and make something out of myself. My love of basketball had not diminished and so I figured out a way to still be close to the game; if I couldn't play for the school's team I would just referee intramural games. Maybe if I stayed diligent and close to the sport, the head basketball coach would give me a second chance.

One evening while I was in the shower in my dorm, one of the baseball players came in and said I needed to come with him. I assumed it was the intramural director wanting me to referee a game. To my surprise, we went straight to the office of the head baseball coach. Coach Frazier was a Hall of Fame coach who had run the baseball program for quite some time at Louisburg and he was known for developing players who would often transfer to prominent university programs or get scouted by major league scouts.

I had no idea why he wanted to see me. I hadn't been recruited out of high school and, to be honest, I hadn't given much thought about baseball since leaving high school. As I walked into his office, Coach Frazier motioned for me to take a seat. I obliged and was curious as to what this was about. Coach Frazier said, "Cordell, I got a phone call from one of my former players, Glen Carr, who coached against your high school team. He informed me that every time they played against Nottoway, you killed them – not only with your bat but also with your speed."

I sat there quietly listening and still trying to process what was happening. A rival coach had actually taken the time to call Coach Frazier about me and I hadn't even played for him – I had played against him! He continued on. "I want you to come out and run, throw, and hit for me but what we really need is speed. Is this something that interests you?"

The only thing I could say was, "Okay."

While I had always wanted to become a professional athlete, becoming a professional baseball player had never crossed my mind. That single conversation changed my whole mindset from that day forward. I could not believe that someone who didn't even know me personally had taken the time to pick up the phone and call Coach Frazier. This gave me a dose of confidence that I hadn't felt since I had won the state championship in high school.

As I walked down to the field, my mind drifted back to the speech I had heard given by that major league scout when I participated in the Pony League World Series: *You have to look like a pro ball player in order to stick out in the crowd.* Back then, I didn't understand what he had meant, but it was all beginning to make sense to me now. I knew I would need to turn ordinary into extraordinary.

On my first day of baseball practice, I was so nervous that I threw up behind the dugout. I had never been nervous when playing baseball before, but the stakes had never been this high either. This was my final shot at getting on track to play sports at the collegiate level, which could lead to a professional level. I started off decent enough, but as the season progressed, I really began to develop as a solid player. I needed to be more than just a solid player, however. Everything I did on and off the field after that was with laser sharp focus and commitment. This focus and commitment paid off. I ended up having an exceptional season on the baseball field as well as a pretty good academic semester. I was on my way!

Chapter 20 ~ The Surprise Visit

Summer 1994

After having what turned out to be an exceptional second year all around, it was time to head back home for the summer. I knew mentally I needed to prepare myself for what awaited me there, but with my renewed sense of energy and confidence, I felt I could take on the world.

Not much had changed in terms of my interactions with my family, but I really hadn't expected anything different. I decided that I would not work at the lumber yard for the summer because I didn't want to jeopardize hurting myself and ruin my chances at continuing along the path I had set out on. So, for the first three weeks, I really didn't do much of anything but sit around the house reflecting on how great of a season I had and how just maybe I had a shot at becoming a professional baseball player.

Never in a million years did I ever think I would be sitting around thinking about the possibility of playing baseball at a professional level. There were definitely not many role models I had seen to let me know that it was even a possibility. Jackie Robinson and Hank Aaron had been trailblazers during their time, but there just weren't many African American baseball players in the lime light during this era. Even so, I allowed myself to revel in the thought that I could become one of those guys.

One late evening in June of 1994, I was sitting on the porch daydreaming about that very possibility and swatting at the mosquitoes buzzing around when I noticed a car pulling into our make-shift driveway. I automatically assumed it was someone looking for Granddaddy to bring him their "numbers." Long before the lottery came along, folks played their own kind of illegal gambling game that was similar to the modern day lottery system. Granddaddy was hot and heavy into running and playing numbers, so it wasn't unusual to see strange cars pulling into the yard at this time of evening.

But as the tall, slender white man wearing a baseball cap began to walk toward me, I quickly dismissed that theory. My next thought was that maybe it was the "insurance man" coming to collect the premium for the policy Granddaddy held. I quickly dismissed that thought, too, since I didn't hear him sprinting out of the back door to avoid him. As the man walked up the steps, he paused and tilted his head toward me with a grin on his face. He reminded me of Clint Eastwood – tall and slinky, walking with an air of confidence. Before he even opened his mouth, I was thinking to myself, *Who is this guy?*

I didn't have to wait long to find out because he walked directly up to me, shook my hand and introduced himself. "Hi, Cordell! My name is Lon Joyce and I'm a scout for the L.A. Dodgers. We drafted you in the 60th round of the 1994 amateur baseball draft."

Everything around me began to move in slow motion. I felt like I was in the twilight zone. Could this be real? Statistically, less than 10.5 percent of NCAA college seniors get drafted by a major league baseball team, and I wasn't even close to being a senior. I had only played one year at the college level, which actually put me in the .5 percent range of being drafted, and yet here was this guy standing there in front of me telling me that I had been drafted. It was in the 60th round, no less, but I was still a draft pick.

Mr. Joyce continued. "We think you have a lot of potential and you show great raw skills. We'd like to see you polish those raw skills with another year in college. Our goal is to draft you higher next year. We will follow you closely. You really have the potential to be a top five pick." In actuality, I had the option of going in at this level, but they had really drafted me to give me an incentive to keep pushing to become a more developed player so that I could be drafted in a higher round the following year if I put the work in.

As I sat and listened to the words that had just come out of his mouth, I was completely dumbfounded. The mosquitoes that had been eating me alive moments before stopped buzzing in order to listen to what he was saying, too. It was as if everything was frozen in time – me, the mosquitoes and his words! I thought the dude must have mistaken me for someone else. I was totally numb, but it was the first time in my life that I went numb for something good. I actually had to pinch myself. And it didn't take me long to make my decision.

I definitely wanted to give myself every fighting chance to be the best, so I decided to forego this draft and wait until the 1995 draft season. He put his hand on my shoulder and with a smile told me, "Keep working hard, son and we look forward to having the opportunity to draft you next year when you are little more developed."

With those parting words, he was gone just as fast as he had come and my world instantly changed. I was on cloud nine, and things were only going to get better.

Chapter 21 ~ The Florida Marlins Workout

About a month after the visit from the Dodgers scout, I got a call from my former high school baseball coach – Coach Wilson. He wanted me to come down to the old baseball field to work out with a scout from the Florida Marlins. This was just too good to be true! As I walked into the stadium, I saw my old coach talking to the scout and he was beaming with pride. As far as I knew, no one in the history of our school had been looked at by a professional baseball scout. I knew I couldn't let him down.

He walked over to me and introduced himself. I don't even remember his name, but I do remember him saying, "I heard you were drafted by the Dodgers in the 60th round. I'm glad you didn't sign with them. Go stretch so we can get to work. We're going to do the 60 yard dash to see your speed and then we are going to do some drills to test your arm strength. We are interested in you, but we feel like you need another year to develop."

I was completely fine with that. I did a quick warm-up and then I was ready to show him my skills. He handed me a wooden bat and it felt like the earth had suddenly stood still. As I stared at this foreign object in my hand, my immediate thought was, "Uh-oh! This is going to be interesting." Not only had I never held a wooden bat, but I'd never seen one in person. I had only seen them on TV while watching Atlanta Braves games. The enormity of the situation sunk in for me at that very moment. These people were actually looking at me as a prospect to play in the Major Leagues!

I quickly refocused. The bat was heavier than I had imagined. It had a completely different feeling than the aluminum bats I had been playing with all of my life. It felt unnatural, but the scout told me that I needed to use it because if I was drafted, this was the type of bat I would be using. I was able to knock balls across the fence at any given time when I used the aluminum bat. I wasn't too sure what I was going to do with this one.

He pitched 125 balls to me that day. I hit two balls out into the outfield and the other 120 were either ground balls or weak fly balls in the infield. Needless to say, he wasn't impressed by my offensive skills, but my speed on defense and on the base pads made him take a second look. He decided to invite me to a camp in Maryland to workout with the rest of the prospects that the Marlins were interested in potentially signing the following year. I was revved up and ready to go!

But my offensive performance at the camp fell short again. I pretty much performed at the same level with the hitting and throwing drills that I had performed for the scout back at my high school, but once again, my speed on defense had piqued their curiosity. They decided to do a speed race with the fastest players. This was my moment to shine because I was well aware that this was my strength.

It came down to me and one other guy in the final race. When the whistle blew, we both exploded out of the stance and we were off. My mind drifted back to John taking my hand in the backyard and running down the hill. There was no way I was going to lose this race. The guy next to me was just as fast as I was, but I was not intimidated by him. This race was mine to win. As we approached the finish line, I gave one last desperate explosion and crossed the finish line. My time was 6.37 seconds. Yes! Then they called out his time: 6.35. NO!!! The better man at that moment had won the race, but I still left on a high. That was my best ever recorded time. I was proud of what I had accomplished and I knew I had a big future ahead of me.

Chapter 22 ~ The Brilliant Idea

Fall 1994

My confidence was at an all-time high. I was finally being recognized for my skills, and it was an awesome feeling. Yet, no one in my family even knew what had transpired that summer. I didn't want the possibility of negativity seeping into my head from what they might possibly say, so I just decided to keep it to myself. I chose, instead, to reflect on everyone who had pushed me to this point: my coaches. In fact, all of my coaches from my little league years - Coach Thomas, Coach Semtner, Coach Adams, Coach Hart and Coach Jones - had all believed in me. They had looked past the raggedy-dressed shy kid and saw a light in me that my family had never bothered to see. All of my coaches from middle school through high school had pushed me even further: Coach Miller, Coach Williams, Coach Boswell, Coach Ingram, Coach Wilson, Coach Harris, Coach Herring and Coach May had given me the support I needed to get to this point. It gave me a sense of empowerment that I had never felt before. I was going to take a proactive approach to ensure I maintained this feeling and made them proud.

So I decided to head back to Louisburg early to check on the status of my classes so that I would know what I needed in order to graduate. To my surprise, the registrar's office informed me that I only needed 18 hours to graduate. At that moment, I came up with what I thought was a brilliant idea. I would move off campus for the fall semester and take classes part-time. My rationale was that since my tuition wasn't being paid by any type of scholarship and I had to take out loans each semester, I could save a lot of money by not taking out such a large loan for the fall semester. I could take classes on a part-time basis and work part-time. Therefore, my intention was to move back to campus for the spring semester and finish up strong with my classes and the baseball season. It all made perfect sense to me.

I set out looking for a job and a place to live. In the meantime, during my search, the intramural director, Big Erv, allowed me to stay in his cottage across the street from the college. In less than a week, I had found a job as a general utility worker, a fancy term for dishwasher and any other grimy task that needed to be done, at the Applebee's located on the NC State campus in Raleigh, North Carolina. This was about a 45 minute commute to and from Louisburg. I also found an apartment in Raleigh directly behind school, but it would be a few weeks before it would be ready. Big Erv was fine with me staying a few more weeks because he knew that it would only be for a short term.

While all of this was transpiring, I had begun talking to a young lady that lived in New Jersey. One of the basketball player's girlfriend had mentioned that she thought we would make a nice couple and had given me her phone number. I never really had a girlfriend because my focus had always been sports, but I was pretty lonely, so I decided to give her a call. We talked on the phone for hours. It felt good to finally have someone I could talk to and seemingly relate to. The fact that we had never met and I was divulging personal information really didn't matter to me at the time. All that mattered was that finally, I didn't feel alone in this world outside of sports.

We talked every day for two weeks straight. On our final conversation, she mentioned to me that she was moving back to High Point, North Carolina with her mom. I was excited about the possibility of finally meeting her, so I told her that she should come by the cottage on her way to High Point. She agreed, and as promised, she dropped by to visit on her way in from

New Jersey. It was a weekend I will never forget. Not for the obvious reasons that you would expect, but for much bigger reasons that would have much larger consequences later on.

After she moved back to High Point, we continued our conversations over the phone for a while, but it really didn't last that long. I had finally moved into my apartment, and I was busy working and traveling back and forth to school. Not to mention the fact that I couldn't afford a phone line in my apartment and nobody had cell phones back then, so I really wasn't talking to *anybody* on the phone. I didn't realize it at the time, but I had begun to lose focus on why I was really there.

Much of my focus was on how I was going to pay the rent and utilities each month. I had gotten myself into a vicious cycle and hadn't even realized it. One night, when I was on my way back from campus, I was involved in a minor accident. I wasn't hurt bad, but I certainly knew I wouldn't be able to make it into work that night, so I called my supervisor and told him I couldn't make it in. Although I had been a hard worker and had never called out, I was told that if I didn't show up that night, I would be fired. Needless to say, I got fired.

Suddenly, I had all these responsibilities I hadn't had a few months before and now I didn't have a job to cover them. I quickly rebounded, though, and found a job at the local Harris Teeter in Raleigh where I worked as a grocery bagger. I fell right in; I even got 'Bagger of the Month' for two months straight and was proud! At that point, it wasn't clicking to me that I had totally lost focus of my goals. Where in the heck had my priorities gone? Although baseball season wasn't until the spring, I should have been focusing on my game and working out in order to develop into the player that the Dodgers scout had been looking for. I also should have been focusing on my classes. The unfortunate fact was that I really didn't have to time to focus on the two most important reasons I was there.

Chapter 23 ~ Bombshell Dropped

I began to feel like I was sinking in quicksand and couldn't get out. I didn't make much being a bagger, so I had to pull extra hours just to cover the rent and all of the gas I was spending on my 45 minute commute between Raleigh and Louisburg. In my infinite wisdom, although I was spending all of this time running back and forth working and paying bills, it wasn't that big of a deal because I was already a shoe-in for the draft the following year.

Well, my days of "no worries" came to an abrupt halt when I got a visit from the same friend whose girlfriend had introduced me to the girl from New Jersey. I heard the words coming out of his mouth, but they sounded completely foreign to me: *"She says she's pregnant and the baby is yours."* It was as if a two-ton weight had been dropped on my head. This could not be happening – not now! He assured me that his girlfriend thought that she was lying and was just probably trying to get back at me because I had stopped calling her.

"Yeah, that was it," I said to myself. Deep down, I knew that probably wasn't the case, but that didn't stop me from quickly taking it as my truth. I was not ready to be anyone's daddy. I obviously was struggling to take care of myself and the thought of having to take care of someone else shook me to my core.

Chapter 24 ~ The Reality Check

Winter 1994

With everything that had transpired in the few short months since I had been back in school, I was physically and emotionally drained. I tried not to think about the possibility of becoming a father, but the thought loomed heavily in the back of my head. In November, Coach Frazier called me into his office to make sure I was going to be returning to campus for the spring semester and returning to the team. He must have sensed that I had lost focus somewhere along the way. I eagerly told him that, "yes," I would be returning to live on campus and, "yes," I was ready to play.

At that point, all I wanted was to put everything that had happened that fall in the past and move on. The problem, however, was that because of everything that *had* transpired, I was neither mentally nor physically ready for the upcoming baseball season. I tried to convince myself that I could get back on top of my game and repeat my level of performance from the prior season. I just needed that edge back. Instead, what I got was a rude awakening.

I was excited to move back onto campus and hit the restart button. As I lay on the bed in my dorm room contemplating the crazy four months I had just endured, there was a knock at the door. It was my friend's girlfriend. I was surprised to see her. But it didn't take me long, though, to figure out what the visit was about. She told me that she had seen her girlfriend recently and she was VERY pregnant and the baby was due very soon. That old feeling of numbness took over my body. I couldn't believe this was really happening. I had tried so hard to convince myself that she really wasn't pregnant.

She had written me a letter a while back, but I had chosen not to read it because I was scared of what it would say. If I didn't read it, it wasn't real.

After shaking up my world with this news, my friend's girlfriend turned and left just as quickly as she had arrived. I decided that now might be a good time to read the letter, and, sure enough, the words on the paper confirmed for me what I had just heard with my own ears and what I had known in my gut all along. What was I supposed to do now? I didn't have anyone to turn to for help. Was I supposed to just settle for a regular job and throw everything away that I had worked so hard to achieve? If I did have someone to talk to that's probably exactly what I would have been told, but I just couldn't see myself giving up now. At that moment, I became more determined than ever to reach my goal of becoming a pro athlete. It was no longer just about me anymore. I was about to be responsible for another life. I needed to make sure I did everything that I could to provide a better life for my child – a life better than the one I had.

Over the course of the first fifteen games of the season, I performed at a level that was nowhere near the caliber of what I had done just one season ago. I had become a shell of my former self on the field. So, I made the decision to focus on two things: my team and my best strength: base running. I was considered one of the leaders of my team and I knew I needed to lead by example. I had to be the stage setter (a term often used in baseball that meant leader) and just get it done. That meant any opportunity I saw to get on base, I was going to take it no matter the cost. My thinking was if I could make something happen, it would be a spark for the rest of my team to follow suit.

The funny thing about baseball, though, and one of the cardinal rules, is that you should never force anything – you should always allow the game to flow naturally. When that flow is interrupted, it usually spells trouble for you and it more often than not puts your teammates in a bad position. This significantly decreases the chances of a positive outcome. It's like a cancer that spreads throughout the team and completely disrupts the momentum.

And that's exactly what happened. I became the cancer for my team. Instead of helping them, I became a detriment to what we were trying to accomplish. We ended up losing in the first round of the conference tournament in Spartanburg, South Carolina. I was completely deflated because I knew that I had a lot to do with our poor performance. I felt like crap. Not only had I let myself down but, I had also let my team down.

One night during the tournament, as I walked back to the bus after an abysmal performance, Lon Joyce, the Dodgers scout who had visited me at my home the summer before, walked up to me. As promised, they (the Dodgers organization) had been watching me closely. Before he opened his mouth, I already had a knot in my stomach. Something told me he wasn't there to be the bearer of good news. "Lon Joyce, of the L.A. Dodgers" he said as he reached out to shake my hand. "You guys had a rough tournament. You don't seem to have gotten better. Cordell, you don't look anything like the player I saw last year. You don't even look like you belong on a baseball field."

His brutal honesty was a shock to my system as I stood there in sheer disbelief. How could it possibly get any worse? But before I could even process what he had just said, the next thing that came out of his mouth solidified that there *was* something worse he could say. "Son, I suggest you finish up school and go ahead and get a job in whatever field you studied in school because you are not going to have a career in baseball."

Those words crushed me to my core. How could I have let my "brilliant idea" and everything that followed in those four short months ruin my dreams? I was pissed off, but I had no one to blame but myself. I had put myself in this situation and I was the only one that could get me out of it. I wasn't ready to call it quits. I knew it would be an uphill battle, but I was determined to become a pro baseball player. I surely had made it harder on myself, but I knew I could push through just as I had always done.

When I got back to campus the next day, I received a phone call from Bethune-Cookman University, a small, four year university in Florida. They told me that they were interested in having me fill the starting position of centerfielder. I knew that since I no longer had a chance at the draft this year, I would need to transfer to a four year university in order to continue to play at the collegiate level. This was the only way I would get another opportunity to prove myself to the major league scouts. I began to seriously consider this option, but my only problem was I wasn't sure if I would actually get the exposure I needed because they were such a small school.

If I was going to get the exposure I needed next year to get the attention of major league scouts again, I knew that I would have to decline the offer from Bethune-Cookman. I knew I had the skills; I just needed a venue to display them. Earlier in the season, a scout from Virginia Commonwealth University (VCU) had come to one of my games. I really didn't give it any thought during that time because I was still thinking I was going to be drafted, so playing for a four year school wasn't even on my radar. Well, now it was the only thing on my radar. VCU was a Division I school and they were pretty well known for their baseball program. I felt they were the best shot I had to reach my potential. I had no idea if they would even be interested in me at this point since I never heard from the scout, but I was going to call them to find out.

I called Assistant Coach Finwood at VCU and asked him if he had remembered seeing me play. He told me that he did remember me, but from what he saw, I was not Division I material. OUCH! In just one season,

I had gone from a 60th round draft pick to not even being considered good enough to play division I college ball. His response was not what I wanted to hear, but I wasn't deterred. I was not going to get off of that phone until I got the answer I was looking for.

I pleaded with him for just one opportunity to show him my real skills. He conceded and told me I could come to a youth baseball camp he was holding for the summer at Fork Union Military Academy. I knew my window of opportunity was closing quickly and I had to jump on it. I was on my way. Now I just needed to graduate or at least I thought that was the only thing I needed to focus on.

On April 28, 1995, at 3am in the morning, I was awakened by a phone call. My boy's girlfriend was on the other line. She was so excited that I could barely understand what she was saying. The only thing I initially heard her say was "Congratulations!" Then she went on to say something about a "baby girl" and a bunch of numbers about weight and height. My only response was, "Oh! Okay, alright." She said congratulations again and then we said goodbye.

As I laid back down, the enormity of everything hit me at that moment. The conversation with Lon Joyce, the phone call from Bethune-Cookman, the phone call to VCU, the necessity of passing my biology course in order to graduate and now a baby. How had I gotten myself so turned around? It was as if I were inside one of those glass snow globes I had played with as a child and someone had just picked it up and shook it as hard as they could, and was watching to see where I'd settle.

Despite everything that was happening, I had to put my energy somewhere positive. I wasn't ready to take on the responsibility of being a daddy, so I held off on going to see my new daughter. I centered all of my energy on the prospect of transferring to VCU in the fall. I knew I would have to eventually face the music and take on my responsibility, but just for a few more weeks, I wanted to pretend everything was "normal."

Chapter 25 ~ The College Graduate

Spring 1995

I was completely psyched that I might have the opportunity to finally transfer to a division I school to play ball. It wasn't the kind of "ball" that I originally thought it would be, but that didn't matter anymore. Football and basketball were a distant memory – baseball was going to be my destiny. I was on cloud nine about the prospect of taking the next step in fulfilling my dreams. Unfortunately for me, my biology professor was about to turn that cloud into a rainstorm.

As I was about to leave class one day, she asked me to stay behind so that she could speak to me. She told me that although I had started off strong at the beginning of the semester, my grades had begun to plummet. I would have to pass the final in order to pass her class. That also meant that if I didn't pass her class, I wouldn't graduate, and if I didn't graduate, I wouldn't be able to transfer to VCU. *Why did I keep putting myself in these predicaments?* But I didn't have much time to think about the answer because I had a biology test to study for – a test that was going to determine what direction my life would go in next.

Although I stayed up all night attempting to study and review my notes, I spent more time thinking about what would happen if I didn't pass. I had no back-up plan. It was do or die – well, not really die, but that's what it felt like. The next day, I stepped into that classroom with a purpose and a focus that I had never had toward my academics. I completed the test and sat around for the next three hours on pins and needles waiting for the grades to be posted. Finally, they were up. As I walked over to the wall where the professor had posted them, it felt like my legs had lead in them. It had never taken me that long to recognize my own name on paper. As I scrolled down the sheet, it felt as if everything around me had slowed down. I finally found my name – *Cordell Farley – Final Grade D*...YES!!!! I had passed! But what was more important was that I was going to graduate from college!

I had been so focused on fixing my mistakes that I had not allowed myself to let the idea sink in that I was actually about to be a college graduate. Although Louisburg was a junior college, meaning it should have only taken me two years to complete, I was finally graduating after three hard, long years. My emotions began to run high. I wanted someone to share in this moment with me and who better than my parents. Maybe I had finally proven myself worthy of their adoration. I called them and told them the date and time of my graduation. I remember they said that they would try to make it. Surprisingly, I was okay with that. If they did come, that was fine. But it they didn't, I knew I would be okay with that, too. I was so used to them not showing up that I didn't put a lot of emphasis on their comment.

When graduation day finally came, I remember scanning the crowds of people in attendance looking for a familiar face, but there were so many people there that it was hard to make out faces. It was such a momentous moment for me to hear my name called as I walked across the stage. And even though it had taken me three years to get my two year degree, it was all worth it. I wouldn't have traded that moment for anything. I felt a sense of relief that I was now a college graduate and no one could take that away from me. I also knew it put me one step closer to fulfilling my real dream.

Immediately following the ceremony, all of the graduates began to look for our families in the thick crowds of people. I knew it would be a challenge to find my family, but that was part of the excitement of the day. After walking around for about a half hour, I finally came to the sinking realization that I would not find them. Not one single soul from my family had come to share in this special day for me. The pain I felt at that moment was excruciating. I know I should have known better, but I had let myself believe for a moment that they really did care about me. Shame on me…

Chapter 26 ~ The Fork Union Camp – Do or Die

Before returning home after graduation, I knew I had somewhere else to be. I finally got up the nerve to go see my new daughter, Marcella. One of my friends from school drove down to High Point with me. At that moment, I had very conflicting emotions. I was kind of excited about seeing her, yet scared about how her mother would react since I hadn't seen her during the entire pregnancy. I also didn't even know if her grandmother would even open the door for me. I had gotten her daughter pregnant and then I had disappeared – I hadn't even met her. The fear of rejection loomed heavily over me, but I knew I couldn't allow these emotions to overtake me because if they did, I knew I would turn around and not face up to my responsibility.

To my surprise, Marcella's mother was pretty cordial considering the circumstances. I held my new daughter for a couple of hours, just staring at her - not saying much. When I finally got up to leave, I turned to Marcella's mother and handed her $80; it was everything I had at that moment. She initially wouldn't accept it, but I insisted and told her that I knew this child was my responsibility and that I would take care of her. I left with a feeling that my life would never be the same. There was no more room for errors or complacency.

A couple of days after I made the visit to Marcella, I returned home where my parents and other family members gave me half-hearted congratulations on my accomplishment of getting my Associates Degree. A normal person would think that since I was the first person in my family to graduate from college, it would be a monumental occasion for everyone. How silly of me to think about what a normal person would think! I had forgotten that they really didn't consider me to be "real" family.

As I stood there in the front living room listening to their less than enthusiastic congratulations, the disconnection that I felt from them highlighted the plight of my earlier years. I didn't even bother to tell them that I was a brand new daddy of a little baby girl in North Carolina. If they didn't accept me as their "real" family, they certainly wouldn't accept her. I decided in that moment as I drudged back toward my old room, dragging everything I owned in a couple of white trash bags, that I would focus all of my energy on the upcoming summer camp at Fork Union where I would have the opportunity to show Coach Finwood my true skills. I had successfully mastered the art of compartmentalizing my feelings and now, more than ever, I needed to implement this skill.

A few days later, upon arriving to camp, I met another recruit, Jamethro, that happened to be from South Hill, Virginia, which was only about 45 minutes from where I grew up. After talking for a while, we realized that although he was a couple of years behind me, we had actually played against each other in high school. He had played two years at a junior college in Maryland and he was now the top recruit for VCU for the outfield position, the position I was trying out for. But he clearly had the advantage. Still, it really didn't bother either one of us because we both respected each other's ability.

During the camp, I was finally able to display the skills that I knew I had, but had not shown during my final year at Louisburg when Coach Finwood had visited. He complimented me on the drastic improvements I had made in the short period of time and told me he was interested in me coming to VCU as a walk on. I remember his words clearly: "Cordell, I can't make any promises, but our program could utilize your speed to be an occasional base runner."

I felt deflated. This meant that I wouldn't be able to display any of the skills I had worked so long to develop. I knew I was so much more than a pinch runner, base runner or whatever you want to call it. Pinch runners didn't make it to the league. I was angry and frustrated at the idea that he had only seen me once and had pretty much relegated me to a utility player. This was not the outcome I had hoped for, but it did present a small window of opportunity that I planned to exploit with everything in me.

Chapter 27 ~ A Whirlwind Year

Fall 1995 – Age 22

Upon arriving at VCU, I knew it would be my final opportunity to prove myself worthy of being pro league material. I could not make the same mistakes that I had made during my final year at Louisburg. My laser-sharp focus had come back with a vengeance. I promised myself that I would eat right, exercise, keep my emotions in check and keep my junk in my pants – basically the opposite of everything I had done the year before. I had to look like a baseball player on and off the field. And I knew that in order to get the attention of head coach Paul Keyes, I would have to put my all in well before the season started. I had squandered a rare opportunity the year before and now I was getting a second chance to prove myself. And I did not let it go to waste.

Although the season didn't start until the spring, we had what was called "fall ball." This was pretty much an opportunity for the younger guys and guys like myself to get in some baseball conditioning before the regular season. I made it a point to come in first during every conditioning drill. I went after every ball no matter how out of reach they seemed to be. We had to be up by 4:15 in the morning three times a week to walk to the gym that was two miles away in order to take an aerobics class. I was never late. We had to go the weight room at least three times a week. I went at least four times a week. I knew I had to separate myself in order to stand out in the crowd and be recognized.

By the end of fall training that November, I had caught the attention of Coach Keyes and had won the starting position for centerfield for the upcoming season. I had worked so hard to get back to this point that by our last scrimmage during the fall, I had completely overworked my legs. I got a base hit and couldn't even run. I had worked so hard that my legs had given out on me. As I prepared to go home for the holiday, I was scared that I would lose my position before I had actually played in a real game. Luckily for me, what I needed was rest and Christmas break after exams provided that needed rest.

When the real season finally started in February, my legs were back at full strength. Unfortunately, we lost the very first game of the season. Coach Keyes gave us a tongue lashing on our trip home. He specifically singled me out.

"Cordell, you looked like you were just happy to make contact with the ball!" he screamed.

Ouch! I promised myself at that moment that I would not let him down again. He had entrusted me with a starting position and I didn't want him to have any regrets about it.

As the season progressed, we really began to mesh as a team and our record reflected our efforts. I played up to my strengths of base hitting and stealing bases. I even broke VCU's record for stolen bases in a single season (a record still held to this day). Midway through the season, I began getting questionnaires from major league scouts. This was exciting, but I knew I needed to stay focused on the team's goals and not my own individual goals. If I stayed focused, everything else would fall into place. And that's just what happened.

During one game against James Madison University, I was up at bat and hit a sharp ground ball back to the pitcher. I was pretty sure that the ball would beat me to first base, but I had promised myself that I would give it my all on every single play. I ran down to first base as fast as I could even though I knew I would be called out. At the end of the game, a scout from the St. Louis Cardinals ran up to me and told me that he had clocked me at 3.2 seconds going to first on that play. He said, "I don't know who you are, but I want to sign you!"

I was completely taken aback and began to stutter, but I quickly caught myself and shut my mouth because I didn't want to sound stupid. I just wanted to take what he was saying in, so I just listened attentively.

He asked, "What is it going to take to sign you?" I didn't know how to answer him and I sensed he knew this. So he continued, "When you figure it out, just let me know. When I like a guy, the organization normally backs me up. I'll be speaking with you soon."

At that moment, I realized that I just might have a real second shot at being drafted again. I also knew that nothing was guaranteed until draft day and I would keep everything in perspective until that day arrived. That conversation took place about a month before the end of the regular season. I just kept plugging away at each game knowing that the prospect of being drafted was high. At the end of the season, Coach Keyes called me into his office.

"Cordell are you planning to return next year?"

While I was thankful for the opportunity he had given me, I knew I couldn't let this bigger opportunity pass me by. I was straight with him and said, "Coach, if I'm drafted, I'm signing."

He responded with a light laugh and said, "You know if you come back next year to play for me, I will make sure you're on full scholarship." The irony was that this was what I had wanted four years ago as a senior in high school, but now I had my eye on another prize. "The buzz is that you are going to get drafted no earlier than the 16th round."

I was okay with that because I knew I it would be the beginning of me controlling my destiny. We shook hands and I walked out of his office. The draft would be in one month and I couldn't wait to see what would happen next.

Chapter 28 ~ The Call

Summer 1996

Ring...Ring...Ring...
Hello...
"Cordell?"
Yes, this is him....
"Good afternoon, this is Scott Nichols of the St. Louis Cardinals. We just wanted to inform you that we drafted you in the 10th Round."

The words that had just been spoken to me over the phone were surreal. I was not present in my body. I had finally accomplished my goal of becoming a professional athlete, but, ironically, none of that mattered in that moment. Although I had been shunned for years by the people that were supposed to love me, all I wanted to do was share this special moment with my family. Logically, I should have been dancing off the walls that the opportunity had finally presented itself to me to walk out of this life and to never look back. Funny thing about humans, though, is that we don't always think with pure logic. Acceptance and appreciation mean more to us than we often realize.

As I sat there and contemplated the news, I knew that no matter how great it was, it didn't mean a hill of beans if there was no one to share the joy with. I may have been professionally ready for this next journey in my life, but was I emotionally ready?

Part II

Chapter 29 ~ And So It Begins

Spring 1996

After the phone call, I just sat on my bed in a daze. The feeling was so surreal. I had finally accomplished the goal that I had set for myself so long ago. I wanted to share this with Granddaddy and Big Ma, but I just didn't want their possible reactions to ruin the moment. So I said nothing.

Days later, as I sat on the porch deep in my thoughts, Granddaddy walked up to me and asked, "So what happened?" I really didn't know what he was referring to since we hadn't had any type of conversation about anything.

"What happened with what?" I replied.

He said, "Baseball."

As I sat there looking at him, the only thing going through my head was, *Why in the hell are you asking me this? Why now? What's the purpose?* I didn't want any extensive conversation with him about this. There was no connection. I just wanted him to go on about his business. But I had to say something, so I finally responded, "The Cardinals picked me up." That was it. He didn't so much as utter a grunt. He just walked away and I was just fine with that.

The only other person I told before I left was Coach Keyes, my coach at VCU. He offered me the scholarship once again, but I declined. He completely understood, though, when I turned him down. He knew that I was starting behind the curve with my age. I was 23 years old and the average first year player was 18 or 19 years old. That's a big difference in baseball years. I didn't care about any of that, though. I just wanted to prove that I had the talent and skills to make it to the big leagues.

The following week, I left for spring training in St. Petersburg, Florida. Regular spring training had already ended and all of the guys that were going to Single A ball all the way up to the big leagues had already left. All of the guys that were in extended spring training and rookie ball were still there. I knew that I would be starting in rookie ball because the season had already started. When I arrived, I checked into the nicest hotel I had ever been in: the Doubletree Hotel. I had stayed in motels before when I went to the Little League World Series, but there was no comparison. The room was huge with the most comfortable pillows I had ever laid my head on. It even had a microwave and refrigerator. But what really topped it off were the warm chocolate chip cookies they had in the lobby – and they were free! This was going to be the life. I finally felt like I mattered.

We were in spring training for two weeks before it was time to head out with my first team. I was sent directly to Rookie Ball in Johnson City, Tennessee. I wasn't sure how it worked with the housing. I just assumed there would be a stipend to take care of this expense. That wasn't the case at all. This was my first reality check in being a professional MINOR league baseball player. It was up to me to find my own place and find one that would fit into my very small budget ($850 a month – before taxes). Five other teammates and I ended up getting a very less than desirable two bedroom apartment in a very less than desirable neighborhood, to say the least.

I had worked so hard to get away from home and "make it," and here I was again sleeping on the floor and surrounded by people I didn't know and had no connection to. Although this was not what I had at all imagined, I knew I had to make the best of it and keep my focus on what was important. This wasn't going to be it for me. I knew there was more and I just needed to push through to get there.

I did really well in Rookie Ball, so much so that I was moved up after about 15 games. My next stop was Peoria, Illinois to low A ball. I was happy to move up, but I was starting all over again. The organization paid my flight to get there, but I was on my own in paying for my hotel and figuring out my living situation. The team consisted of mostly white and Latino guys, and within each group, they seemed to look out for each other. There was only one other black guy on the team other than myself, so I thought it was a safe bet to ask him about housing. I asked if I could sleep on his floor until I could find a place since the hotel was $100 a night and we were all in pretty much the same boat (or so I thought). He said his father was paying his rent and promptly told me NO. I forgot to mention we were playing the same position. So much for camaraderie and solidarity.

For the next five nights, I stayed in the $100 night hotel. That was $500 gone in the blink of an eye. In addition to my monthly check of $850, I had gotten a $10,000 signing bonus when I was drafted, but the way things were starting, I had a feeling it wouldn't last long. Boy was that an understatement! No one told me that I should probably open a checking account and surely this was something I hadn't been taught at home, so I carried the $10,000 in cash around with me. Well, all of it except about $750. I put that in my suitcase.

After returning from a game one night, I looked in my suitcase and discovered that the $750 was missing. I immediately called down to the front desk to report the theft. The police were called and they came to do an "investigation." The next day, I got a call back from the police department stating that their "investigation" came up empty. They then proceeded to ask me if I was sure I hadn't gotten drunk and spent all of it down at Big Al's strip club. I was dumbfounded and completely pissed. I hadn't been in this town even three days yet and I had been robbed and accused of being a drunk.

I told one of my teammates about what happened and he suggested I go meet with his broker to invest some of my money. I eagerly accepted and met up with him a day later. I invested $2,500 with him to put into stocks. What that meant, I didn't have a clue, but it seemed like the sensible thing to do at the time.

A couple of days later, we finally went on the road to play, which saved me some money because the team would pay our hotel bills while we were on the road. When we returned, I played a few more games before being pulled up to Single A ball. Where I stayed for those few games is still, honestly, a blur. I do remember sleeping on quite a few floors, but it didn't matter because I was on my way back to St. Petersburg, Florida.

When I reached St. Petersburg, I was on a high. The path was I taking was not a normal one. It normally took guys - on average - two years to get from Rookie Ball to Single A ball and I had done it within one season. I think the organization wanted to push this fast because of my age (like I said, I was older than most) and my raw talent. I could only make this assumption since I didn't have anyone representing me or talking to me about what was happening. I was just being shuffled from city to city and I was definitely down for the ride.

However, everything came to a screeching halt in St. Petersburg. It was like I had hit a brick wall. My first game was a total bust. I had pretty much just stepped off the plane and had to head straight to the field to get ready for that night's game with my new teammates. My first at bat, I struck out BIG and it only went downhill from there. For the rest of the season, I only had 3 more at bats and my batting average suddenly plummeted to .000. The team was in a playoff chase and I was not fitting into their flow. I sat out the next 25 games until the season was over.

The organization made a strong suggestion that I begin working on switch hitting, something I had absolutely no experience doing. Although I was left–handed, I batted right. It had honestly never been on my radar to hit left. The organization obviously had a different plan for me and it was one that I was uncomfortable making an adjustment to. I had been promoted twice in one season and suddenly I would have to start all over again from the bottom doing something I had never even conditioned for. At my age, I knew it was going to be an uphill battle. You typically need about 2,000 at bats to be considered a developed professional player. I hadn't had any at bats with my left hand and only 200 at bats with my right hand during the first season. This change basically set me back about four years.

Right before leaving St. Petersburg, I met up with my broker again. He told me that he had pulled the money back out of the stock because he didn't trust that particular stock. My money had already plummeted to $1,800 in those two short months. He handed me the note for the $1,800 and told me it was just like cash. My mind was really on the horrible season I had just finished up and I really hadn't heard anything he told me. This is probably why I threw it away as I was packing up to leave for what had turned out to be a quite an abysmal trip.

I flew back home feeling disillusioned and disappointed. What had originally began as a great first season of my professional career, ended up being a total letdown. Upon reflection, what I realized was that I didn't understand the "culture" or "rules." I had been thrown into a situation where everyone was expected to know what to do and most guys had someone coaching them on what to do if they didn't know. I realized that most of my teammates were represented by an agent or they had a former coach or family member that they could converse with to help them understand what was expected of them. I didn't have that. No one was there to tell me that I should have been preparing for a marathon and not a sprint. I had approached that first season like I approached sports in high school: by going in, pushing hard every day and I had quickly burnt myself out. I didn't understand why I was hitting a brick wall until the season was over. Once again, that feeling of loneliness had found its way right back into my spirit.

During that first offseason, I was totally deflated. I worked out, but I was pretty much going through the motions. I had no focus. I had no guidance. I had no direction. Again, I was frustrated because I seemed to be on the cusp of doing something great, but I didn't know the "rules" or the "culture" and I didn't have anyone to help me figure it out. I was back in Blackstone in the same house, in the same poisonous environment. The old feelings of despair and abandonment seemed to be licking their chops to devour me once again.

I couldn't let this happen. As I sat in my room one day, I actually contemplated ending it all. I would have rather died than to allow the old feelings to once again consume me. I had to make a decision right then and there: end my life or have the courage to move forward and address my fears. At the time, the easiest answer seemed to be to end it all. But I was never one to choose the easy route. I chose life.

A couple of weeks after being at home, I knew I had to get out of the house. I had worked out several times at one of the local YMCA's in Richmond while I was still at VCU and I remembered they had a before and after care program. I figured I would give it a shot to see if I could work there in the mornings and afternoons, and work out in between. When I was in high school, I couldn't pay anybody to give me a job, but now that I was professional athlete, I got a job on the first try and the same day. I spent the rest of the offseason working and working out at the YMCA.

On that first Thanksgiving back home, I decided to take a trip to High Point to see my daughter. She was now one and I really hadn't spent much time with her at all. I spent the day playing with her and visiting with her grandmother. I had only been to see her a few times in that first year, but each time I had gone down there, I had slowly built a cordial interaction with her grandmother. It was rather awkward with her mother and she would normally leave the house when I came, but my daughter's grandmother and I would sit at her kitchen table for hours making small talk.

I returned down there a few weeks later right before Christmas to drop off a couple of gifts for my daughter and to spend a little more time with her because I knew I would be leaving soon for spring training. Although I really didn't know what to do with her whenever I did visit, I wanted to make a concerted effort to be there for her.

One other major event happened that first offseason as well. I finally told Big Ma and Granddaddy about my daughter. Surprisingly, they said, "Are we going to meet her?"

I was totally taken aback by this and really didn't know how to respond, so I just said, "I'm not sure." The conversation was left right there and I didn't speak to them about her again for quite some time.

Chapter 30 ~ The Purge

Before I knew it, it was time to head back to spring training for my second year. I arrived in St. Petersburg for training knowing that I was fighting for my life. My focus had gone from making it to the big leagues to just making it as a human being. The organization's focus was to make me a switch hitter. This was a skill that normally took years to develop and they wanted me to have it now. I had asked myself often during the offseason why was this so important. It was not my strength and it totally took away from my natural skills. So I was now not only fighting for my life, but fighting to stay in the game. I thought I would have a chance to work on some of the fundamentals that other guys had been exposed to in high school, but I had to focus on learning a new skill while fighting the demons of self-loathing that were trying to take over me.

My play suffered tremendously. During spring training, I went from Single A ball to ending up staying behind for extended spring training. I was right back where I had started when I was first drafted. Here I was at 24 years old playing with and against 18 and 19 year old kids.

It was custom for a sports psychologist to come and do an assessment on all of the guys left behind for extended spring training. I guess the organization figured that there must be outside factors affecting their play and the psychologist would be able to figure this out. I was assigned to speak to one. The process began with a long, drawn out, redundant pen and paper questionnaire. There were about 160 questions that seemed to ask the same questions over and over again, but just in a different way: Do you love yourself? Do you like the color yellow? Do you love your father? Do you and your father talk?

I labored through it question by question. Once the paper assessment was over, if everything seemed in order, you were pretty much done. But that was not the case with me. I was called to have a one-on-one session with the sports psychologist because there seemed to be some "inconsistencies" with my answers.

As I sat down in his office, I was totally numb. I just wanted to get it out of the way. My expectation was to answer his questions, interact with him just as I had done with any other stranger in my life and just move on.

He began by explaining to me that my questionnaire had some discrepancies and it was no big deal; he just wanted to clear them up. He went directly into asking me about my relationship with my parents. I astutely answered him by telling him that I was adopted, but everything was good. He then proceeded to ask me about my relationship with the people who raised me (same question, just different wording). Again, I said everything was fine and just tried to blow it off. He then wanted to know specifically how my relationship was with my adopted mother. I told him she was a strong woman and that we were okay. His next question was of the same nature: "How is your relationship with your adopted dad?"

Once again, I glossed over the question with a generic answer. He moved on to the next question, but then circled right back around to another question about my dad. As I began to answer, something took over me and I completely fell apart. I was able to murmur only a few words before totally losing it. I cried uncontrollably for what seemed like an eternity. Everything that had ever happened to me was unmasked and the numbness was lifted. There was a sense of relief from all of the pain, the anger, the frustration, the lies and the cover-up about who I really was. In that moment, I let myself mourn for all of the bad things that had ever happened to me. It was such a relief to finally feel like it was okay to do so.

When I left his office, I felt as if a weight had been lifted from me, a weight that I hadn't even realized I had been carrying for so many years. I had a sense of renewed energy in moving forward. It was what I needed at this very critical point in my personal life and in my professional career. The void was still there, but it was a euphoric feeling to feel "light" and a sense of relief. Although I never went back to see him again, that one visit had peeled back layers of hurt and buried emotions. It was something that had been long overdue and I was somewhat grateful it happened when it did.

Just prior to meeting with the sports psychologist, I had spent a lot of energy working on my arm strength and learning to switch hit so much so that I had begun to lose my instinctual skills. I couldn't even steal a base or catch a routine fly ball. All of my energy had gone towards trying to please the organization without really knowing what it was they wanted from me. I wasn't being allowed to develop and grow in the way I thought I needed to, but that really didn't matter. I was on the verge of being out because not only was I not developing the way I needed to as a switch hitter, but the things that had initially impressed the organization were failing, too.

All of this changed after what I call my purge with the psychologist. I had a renewed sense of myself. I felt like a brand new person. I set out in my mind to showcase who I really was on the field. I was no longer interested in trying to develop as a switch hitter. I was ready and had the self-confidence to show my actual skill set even if it was contrary to what the organization was looking for. I had to be me; it was the only way I was going to survive.

I began to develop solid skills that complimented my natural ability for the rest of the extended spring training. I became aggressive at everything I did. I no longer stepped to the plate as a passive player who was just happy to be there. I became a formidable force on the field. At the end of spring training, I was sent back to

Rookie ball, but I was only there for two weeks before I was sent up to Single A ball, which by this time had been moved from St. Petersburg to Prince William, Virginia. Here was my chance again to prove I was good enough. I had a first great game and it continued from there. I ended up having a solid year in Prince William.

My manager had pushed for me to go to winter ball to further improve my skills, but the organization wasn't interested, so once again, I headed back home. I wanted my own place, but I just couldn't afford it. Any extra money I did have, I sent to my now two-year-old daughter to help support her. The money from the signing bonus was long gone and my paychecks from the season had been used to pay for housing and to try to keep up with my child support payments.

Sadly, many people make the assumption that if you're a professional athlete, you have a fat bank account. That was far from the truth for most minor league baseball players. The benefits are great, but the paychecks were small. I could barely make ends meet when I was a player, but it really wasn't about the money for me. I knew that if I stayed consistent with it, then one day, it would pay off. Unfortunately for me at the time, the child support enforcement agency didn't see it that way and they pretty much took most of what I made and that still wasn't enough.

Still, I did what I could to try and make up the difference. During the season, on away trips, we would get a food stipend of $15 a day. Instead of spending that money on food, I would try and save most of it to send towards my child support. I would keep a few dollars of it and happily take a trip to Wendy's to visit their famous $1 menu while my teammates often ate at nice sit-down restaurants. I was cool with that, though, because it's not like I had been accustomed to that lifestyle anyway.

So, now that the season was over, I knew I would have to quickly find a way to get the funds flowing for the offseason. At the same time, I didn't want to put myself back in the mental state of years past by going back to my old house, so I went to the extreme and lived out of my truck. I didn't want and couldn't afford any distractions. I spent most of my time working at the local YMCA in Richmond again and spent the rest of my time working out. I needed to be ready when I headed back to spring training again.

But right before I headed back to spring training, a former local sports news reporter approached me about signing on with him to represent me as his agent. I really didn't know much about how this worked, but I had seen other guys with agents who spoke to the organization on their behalf, so I figured it wouldn't hurt. At this point, I felt I needed someone to speak for me because I couldn't go directly in to speak with management about my future. I didn't know what to expect heading back to spring training, so I was hoping the agent would help to give me some insight on what the organization was thinking.

Chapter 31 ~ New Game: Politics

When I arrived back to spring training that March, it appeared that my diligence during that off season had paid off because I was immediately sent to train in AAA. I had a couple of good games, but for some reason, they dropped me back down to Single A ball. I was perplexed and decided to call my "so called" agent to find out what was happening. It took him a couple of days to even return my initial phone call and then another couple of days to get back to me with an answer. When he did finally call back, he nonchalantly told me that the organization was beginning to question if I was a good fit for them and word was spreading that they were mulling over the idea of releasing me. I was no longer considered a "hot prospect." He then promptly hung up the phone without any guidance or direction as to what I should do next.

How could this happen so fast when I had just gotten back to spring training and was performing so well? And who was this churl that was supposed to be *vested* in my best interest? I didn't have time to worry about him because I knew I would have to once again "go to bat," so to speak, for myself. I decided that I was going to just go all out and do whatever it took not to be cut. I had nothing to lose.

My first at bat during spring training in Single A ball was a homerun. Suddenly, they took notice again. I performed exceptionally well throughout spring training in Single A ball. That didn't matter, however, when it came to what was known as the "cut days." Cut day was near the end of spring training when most of the big league guys had already left. During this time, instructors and managers would ride about the fields in a golf cart while we worked out and would call guys to go for a "ride" to see management. We knew once a guy took that "ride," he was toast.

Also, during the last part of spring training, the organization had a habit of bringing in a lot of guys that hadn't previously been there throughout training. Most of them were black. They were used as "fill-ins" after the big league, AAA and AA guys had already left. Everybody wanted a chance, but I think the organization knew most of them wouldn't get it. By the time spring training was over, most of them would be cut.

It really messed with my psyche to watch these guys get sliced day in and day out. I was only one of a few black players in the organization, and to watch these guys, some of them real prospects, be used as pawns was difficult. I had come in with the mindset that displaying your talents, consistently putting up good numbers and acting like a pro were the primary criteria required to make it to the big leagues. Sadly, I was quickly learning that talent wasn't as big of a factor as politics. I would soon find out just how political things could get and the adjustment I would have to make in order to mentally and emotionally sustain when I arrived for my first full season of Single A.

The season actually turned out to be one of my best seasons yet. Ironically, it had less to do with what I did on the field and more so with what I did off the field. There was a guy that played the same position as me that the organization considered to be a prospect and they decided to play him in front of me. In all actuality, he was popping steroids left and right because he knew if everything were based on talent alone without the help of steroids, I could beat him any day of the week. In fact, I could still beat him even with his steroid advantage, but I wasn't given the opportunity. The organization, of course, didn't know he was popping pills and, frankly, no one was paying attention. They just wanted to see him perform. It didn't matter that I was better. This was the politics of the game.

So while I waited on the sidelines for my opportunity, I knew I needed to take some of my energy and put it to good use. I needed to be exceptional on and off the field. This is when I really began to get involved with the community of Prince William. I knew that baseball wouldn't last forever. I also knew that at some point in my life, I wanted to be able to add value to the lives of others and be a positive influence.

I had never immersed myself within a community before because I had never stayed long enough in one place to do so, but I now had the opportunity. Every promotional event that the organization had in the community, I was the first to volunteer. I would do guest appearances at the mall, hospital visits, car washes and school functions. I even went as far as dressing up as the team mascot for field day for one of the local elementary schools. That wasn't my most pleasant experience (the kids spent most of the day trying to rip my head off). But it was one of the most memorable.

As I attended these functions, I began to become more comfortable with myself. Each day as I headed to the field for practice, I knew I had to do something to keep up the positive energy while I anxiously awaited my turn behind a steroid junky. My motto of "This Too Shall Pass" didn't quite fit my current circumstances, but there were two new ones that did. My new mantras became: "Only God can judge me" and "Only the strong survive." I took a permanent marker and wrote these words on my game cap. These were the words that would carry me through until I got my chance again.

And it soon came when the guy in front of me blew out his elbow. His steroid use had finally caught up with him and I was waiting in the wings to strut myself. He wished me luck and I remember telling him, "Don't worry. You ain't never getting this spot back."

Despite not really being a factor for the first quarter of the season, I ended up getting Offensive Player of the Year and made the All-Star Team for the Carolina League. By this time, I had also fired my old agent and had acquired a new one who really did seem to have my best interest at heart. He actually communicated with the organization about my interests. He told me that the organization was ready to make a real commitment to me and that I would get a chance to play winter ball. This was the opportunity that I needed to catch up and really develop the skills I had been lacking in order to get over the hump of making it to the big leagues. I was excited, but I didn't want to get my hopes up too high because I had learned that things could change in a heartbeat. But a visit from the General Manager (GM) of the organization certainly did the trick to confirm what I was hoping.

One night after the game, the GM corralled a small group of us by the bullpen to express the organization's acknowledgment of our individual performances that season. He wanted to commend us and let us know that we were representing the organization and our individual performances had been duly noted. He singled me out and said, "I know for some of you it would be great to get some extra work in, isn't that right, Cordell?"

I enthusiastically replied, "Yes, sir!" I knew he was referring to winter ball and I couldn't have been more excited. My time was coming.

There were only a few games left in the season after the GM's visit, so I was anticipating my agent contacting me to give me the details of winter ball. By the last game of the season, that call hadn't come and I was completely perplexed. Hadn't my agent told me they were going to send me to winter ball? Hadn't the GM of the organization (not of the team, but of the entire organization) confirmed with me that I was going? What could have happened in that short period of time? Was anybody even going to bother to tell me?

I eventually got my answer when one of my teammates from the Dominican Republic received a letter confirming he would be going to winter ball. I knew this meant that I wouldn't be going because he and I played the same position. No rejection letter. No sit down meeting to explain the reasoning behind the decision. Not even a slight afterthought comment in passing from anyone in management. Just silence. Once again, I seemed to be so close to getting what I needed only to be shot down at the last moment. For some reason, the organization would not make that commitment to me. This was something I was used to, though, so I shrugged it off and headed back home again for the off-season determined not to give up – but not before I drove that same teammate to Delaware to begin his season in winter ball.

Why would I do that? He had just taken my position from me and, in turn, taken my opportunity. For some reason, I didn't process it that way. For me, he hadn't done any of that. It was the organization who made the decision. He was not from the U.S., he didn't know the language well and he was only trying to make it just like me. He had asked and I obliged. And then I headed back to Blackstone – again.

Initially, when I found out that I wasn't going to be playing winter ball, as I said, I shrugged it off. I was used to rejection and my first instinct was to go into my state of numbness. This had always protected me in the past. I knew, however, that it was time for me to allow myself to feel this pain so that it wouldn't consume me. I really had to start processing what was happening. There was a reality starting to play out that I never imagined I would have to face.

Although I knew the organization had a high regard for my work effort and commitment to the game, I began to realize that it was very well possible that they had no plans to have me be a part of the "bigger picture." And I wasn't going to allow this to consume me. I had just had the best season of my career and I felt good about where I was in my development as a potential big league player. The funny thing is that for the first time in my life, it was of no consequence to me as to whether or not I ever played major league baseball. I was finally taking control of my own life and I wanted to be the best I could be regardless of what happened and it felt great.

This new attitude began to display outwardly. I finally had a little "swagger" in me and although there was still a void in my life, I now smiled because I felt good instead of smiling to mask the pain of my life. This newfound swag could not have come at a better time. My life was about to go into a whirlwind and I didn't even see it coming.

Chapter 32 ~ Fate

Not long after I came back home for the offseason, I connected with the YMCA again and got my position back so that I could make a little money and, at the same time, focus on my offseason workout regimen. I had also begun to clean a couple of million dollar homes in the VCU area. The previous offseason, I had spent some time at the gym by VCU and had met a woman who worked out at the gym and lived in one of these fancy homes. I ended up babysitting for her a couple of times and now decided to reach out to her again during this offseason. She mentioned that she and a couple of her friends were looking for someone reliable to clean their houses and I quickly volunteered my services. I had been cleaning all my life, so I figured, why not get paid for it?

I rotated between cleaning houses, working at the YMCA and working out. I figured the more of my time that was occupied, the less time I would have to spend at home, although, in actuality, over the past two years during the offseason, things had become pretty cordial between me and Big Ma. I had finally come to a good place with her and was gaining a peace within my own self about what had happened between us. As an adult, I had begun to look at her through a very different lens and I saw all of the weight she had been carrying by having the burden of taking care of so many people. This different perspective that I had allowed to start seeping into my spirit only facilitated the healing process that had begun within me.

However, my feelings towards Granddaddy hadn't changed much. He still didn't have much to say to me, nor I to him. One would think that since I was now actually a professional baseball player that he would want some type of acknowledgment and involvement with me and what I had going on, but he really didn't – and I was fine with that.

Even though a lot of the tension had subsided within the house, most of the time I either stayed with one of my old teammates from VCU or I would just sleep in my truck. There were also a couple of other places I laid my head, but no more than a night because I really wasn't interested in any type of relationship at that point (or at least that's what I thought). Occasionally, I would visit with my daughter. By this time, she was three years old. During the course of those three years, my interactions and relationship with her mother was strained and practically nonexistent. Somehow, in my mind, this justified my infrequent visits to see my daughter. But deep down inside, I knew I wasn't putting forth my best effort. It just seemed easier to put my focus on what I knew: baseball. When I wasn't working, working out, visiting my daughter in North Carolina or bouncing from spot to spot in Richmond, I would head back home on the weekends and sit around and watch football to clear my head or go to the club with old friends.

A popular hangout (really the only hangout) was a local club called The Country Inn. Most everyone would go here to hang out, dance and to just have a good time. On weekends, it was the regular locals mixed in with people who were just back home visiting. It was completely insane during the holidays, though, because that was when everybody came back home and they would make their way there because they knew they would run into old friends. That Thanksgiving, I was back in Blackstone for the weekend and decided to call some of the fellas to hang out for the night. As soon as we walked through the door, I headed for the dance floor. I didn't bother to ask anyone to dance because I was perfectly content with getting my groove on by myself. I also knew I was broke and if I asked anyone to dance, they would eventually expect me to buy them a drink, which would lead to some frustration on her part and pure embarrassment for me.

But I did have a little change in my pocket that night and decided to go to the bar to buy myself a drink. As I was waiting, I happened to notice a young lady that I had gone to high school with. Her name was Latrice Hawkes. She had been the head cheerleader when we were in high school, but we never really had any interactions with each other. That night, as she turned to look my way, I thought to myself, *Hmm! She looks good.* She smiled and nodded to me and then nodded toward the dance floor. We danced to every fast song that night and had a complete blast. It was such a euphoric feeling to have that much fun with no expectations on either side. Nothing had ever felt that natural before, but I really didn't think anything of it at the time. At the end of the night, we simply said goodbye and went our separate ways.

By the time Christmas rolled around a few weeks later, I decided to head back to the club again. I had been working hard at the YMCA and with my workout, and I just needed to wind down and have a good time. As luck or fate would have it, my dance partner was there again. She had come back from Charlotte, North Carolina to visit her family for Christmas and had made her way back to the club again, too. Once again, we hit the dance floor and stayed there all night. At one point, one of my friends walked up and said, "You guys would make a cute couple." We both gave him the side eye and started laughing, especially since we had no other connection except dancing with each other that night and at the previous party.

At the end of the night, as she and her friend were walking to the parking lot, I decided at that moment that I wanted to connect with her again. As I walked her to her car, I told her she should give me a call sometime.

She looked at me incredulously and said, "Umm, YOU can call ME."

I was feeling pretty fearless and confident that night, so I playfully asked her if she were "too good to call a brother." I think she took it as a challenge and, to my surprise, she said okay and then pulled away.

The next day, I was outside playing basketball when my nephew, Mary's son, called to me to let me know I had a phone call. I just assumed it was one of my boys calling to see if I wanted to hang out again. To my surprise, it was her on the other end of the line asking me if I was surprised that she had called. I was in total shock, but I couldn't let her know that, so I played it off and said that I wasn't surprised at all. Before she could tell I was shaking on the other end of the phone, I asked her if she was interested in hanging out that evening. It wasn't much to do in our town, so she suggested that we head to one of her friend's house to play cards. We met at one of the gas stations and rode over together. We hung out over there for a few hours and then I took her back to her car. We ended up sitting in the parking lot in my car talking until almost 4 in the morning. I don't think either one of us wanted to end our conversation, but she had to drive back to Charlotte later that day.

As I walked her to her car, I gave her a hug and a kiss on the cheek and said, "Miss Hawkes, I had a great time."

She seem flattered by the comment and quickly responded, "I had a great time, too."

As she was getting in her car, she suddenly paused and looked back over to my car as I was about to get in. She hesitated and then said, "Hey! Do you remember my cousin Duan?"

"Yes," I replied.

She continued on, "Well he's getting married next week on New Year's Eve. Do you want to go with me?"

I was floored, but once again, I played it cool and said, "Yeah, sure."

We agreed that we would connect in a few days when she came back to Virginia from Charlotte. Up until that point, I hadn't exactly been on a lot of "real dates." I never really had an interest, but, for some reason, I was intrigued by this young lady and I was excited about the idea of hanging out with her again.

I spent that week leading up to New Year's Eve working hard between cleaning houses and working at the YMCA. It didn't dawn on me to call her to confirm that we were still, in fact, on for the wedding. I was too busy trying to make sure I had enough money for gas to pick her up and make the drive to the wedding. I didn't have a cell phone anyway, so I was crossing my fingers that she would reach out to me again – even though the only number she had for me was in Blackstone and I hadn't been there all week.

We didn't end up speaking until late afternoon on the day of the wedding. When I got to Blackstone that day, Granddaddy told me that the same young lady had called me a couple of times that week. He butchered her name, but I knew exactly who it was and immediately went to call her to let her know I would be picking her up in a couple of hours. Luckily for me, I was able to get in touch with her just in the nick of time (she later told me that since she hadn't been able to reach me, she had called her best friend to meet her at the wedding and was just about to leave when I called).

The stars had definitely lined up for me on this one. We had a really good time at the wedding and ended up sharing our first kiss later that night. She only had a few more days before she had to head back to Charlotte, but we both knew there was a strong connection between us that neither of us wanted to let go. We decided (I don't know even remember if it was a conscious decision or natural one) to spend every moment she had left in town together.

On one particular night while she was still in town, we got stuck in a snowstorm in Richmond. One of my buddies was out of town and he told me we could stay at his apartment because it was far too dangerous to drive back home. As we sat and talked that night, for the first time, I revealed to her (to anyone for that matter) my feelings of despair from my childhood. I really didn't go into a lot of detail, but I felt comfortable enough with her to let her know that I had always felt a void in my life. She asked me if I would allow her to fill that void. This gesture toward me sealed the deal that she would forever be my lifelong partner.

She headed back to Charlotte a couple of days later, but the distance didn't seem to matter because it felt like we were inseparable. We talked on the phone every chance we could get between her job and my "jobs." We also made plans for when we would see each other again. A couple of weeks into the New Year, I headed to Charlotte to visit her for the weekend. We had an awesome time the entire weekend and although we didn't do much, everything just felt right.

When it was time to leave, I didn't want to go, but I knew I had to get back to my routine of working out, making a little money at the gym and cleaning houses. There was one major problem that I didn't foresee coming, though, that would put a kink into my plan. My good 'ole faithful Bronco decided it wasn't going to start. I couldn't believe I had come all the way to Charlotte and it decided it was going to act up. I was hoping it was just the battery because I knew I could foot the bill for that. I calculated the cost quickly as I sat there turning the key to no avail. I knew I had enough money to get it towed, get a new battery and still have enough money for gas to get back to Virginia. That would have been just too easy, though, and nothing in my life ever seemed to come easy.

After having it towed to a local shop, Latrice took me to the shop to see what was wrong with my truck. As the guy at the shop began rattling off everything that was wrong, I became numb. I really didn't hear anything he said except the part about it was going to cost $900 to fix. I was speechless and embarrassed because I knew I didn't have that kind of money. Without a second thought, Latrice looked at me and said, "I'll take care of it."

Did I mention that she also promptly told me that she had never paid for anything for a guy and that I would be paying her back? In that moment, she was able to immediately take away the shame I was feeling and also put a smile back on my face because I knew she was going to be a feisty one – and I liked it...damn! I think I loved it! A few days later, my truck was repaired and, unfortunately, I had to head back to reality, but I now had something to look forward to other than just getting back to baseball. I couldn't wait for her to come back to Virginia to spend some more time with me.

A couple of weeks later, she said she was coming to Virginia for the weekend to visit and I felt like a kid on Christmas Eve waiting for her arrival. She decided to drive straight from work and head to my house in Blackstone. I knew she was tired when she got there and told her she could lay down on my bed to rest while I washed her truck for her. She looked at me like I was crazy. As I said before, we lived in a small town and everybody knew everybody. She remembered that as a little girl, my mom always looked really mean, not to mention that I had told her that one time when a girl from college had unexpectedly "popped in" to visit me, Big Ma had gone completely ballistic. She didn't particularly care for her (to put it kindly) and promptly told me that she was going to the store, and when she got back home, "that b**ch had better be out of my house."

Then there was the visit to my house a few weeks prior during the holidays when Latrice hadn't actually met my mom, but rather had heard her cussing at me about turning up the heat. So, I guess it was kind of easy to discern why she was a tad bit unsettled about going to my room to lie down. I finally convinced her that it was okay and she nervously went back there to lie down while I went outside.

A funny thing happened, though, while I was outside; she and Big Ma had connected. Big Ma had come into the room while Latrice was lying down and she immediately popped up like a spring when Big Ma walked in. But she immediately put Latrice at ease by asking, "You're Kermit's daughter, aren't you?"

As I said earlier, Big Ma had been known back in the day to have big card games all weekend, every weekend, and it just so happened that Latrice's dad had been one of the regulars at the games. It was like there was an instant connection for Big Ma to Latrice because of her dad, even though there was still no real connection to me. I actually thought it was pretty cool to see them interact and connect. It felt good to see someone I was now connected to be accepted by Big Ma. In a way, it was acceptance for me, too.

I spent the rest of the offseason working out, spending time with Latrice in Charlotte and working. I also introduced Latrice to my daughter during one of my weekend trips to Charlotte. It was important to me that she was not only okay with the idea of me having a child, but also with the fact that we came as a package deal. She never even flinched at the idea. My daughter was still living in High Point and it was only a short drive from Charlotte. So, we picked her up and took her to Chuck E. Cheese, and they immediately hit it off. For once in my life, everything seemed to be falling into place with me personally, but I still needed to gain a sense of where I was going professionally.

As I headed back into spring training that year, I prepared myself for the hard work and the intense focus I would need to get to the next level. Spring training went well and when the season started, I immediately started off in AA. My hard work was finally starting to pay off.

I felt as if my performance from the prior year would get the organization to recognize that I belonged at this next level. It didn't go that way at all, however.

Once again, I was not put in the lineup on a regular basis. Even my teammates came to my defense and questioned why I wasn't playing consistently. They seemed to recognize my skills, but the organization didn't seem to or just refused to. I would have a few good games and start to get into a rhythm, but if I had one bad game, I was immediately benched. Typically, in baseball, players are given the opportunity to work through their struggles without a stop in their flow. For some reason, I wasn't given this opportunity, and I began to become more and more frustrated. I knew this wasn't healthy, so once again, I put my energy into doing appearances and community service projects for the organization. This helped keep my psyche in check so that when the opportunities arose for me to be in the lineup, I would be able to focus.

At some point in the season, I was on a hot streak and was able to stay in the lineup consistently. This paid off for me because, somehow, I made the All-Star team for the AA Texas League. It was a total shock since I really hadn't played that much, but it was a welcomed surprise. After the All-Star break, I felt pretty confident that I would get the chance to play on a consistent basis for the rest of the season. I mean, the league recognized my talent. The organization had to recognize it now, right? No!

When I got back after the break, things went back to the same helter-skelter play time. There were nights after games that I was just ready to pack my bags and call it quits. Day in and day out, I would go into the hot sun and practice all day only to be disappointed when I checked the lineup for the game that night and would not see my name. The same feelings of rejections I had felt as a child were steadily creeping up on me again, but I just refused to accept them.

However, I believe that at some point, I unconsciously stopped giving my all; why should I when they didn't seem to give a damn about me? By the time the season ended, I had begun to question if this was what I really wanted. But what else could I do?

During the offseason, I put all of my energy and focus on what made me happy and feel good, and that was Latrice. By this time, she had moved back to Virginia so that we could be closer when I came home for the off-season. I proposed to her that December and we got married the following February. She was also carrying my first son by the time we got married and I was beyond thrilled. I began to shift around what was important to me and for the first time, sports was no longer at the top of my list. I wanted to be a good husband to my wife, a better father to my daughter and a real father to my yet to be first-born son. I had to make it a priority to make sure they would never have to feel the things I felt growing up. But the only thing I knew at this point was baseball, so I decided I would give it my all again for the upcoming season and see what happened.

I headed back to Arkansas for the 2000 season to play in AA again. It was quite a year of reflection given the fact that I was pretty much a spectator and cheerleader for my teammates. Yet despite this fact, I continued to push and work hard on my skills and my game. I believe at one point during the season, I went almost 40 games without playing a full game. One night in particular, I broke down after coming home. I hated the organization and I wanted out. I came up with all the reasons why it was their fault that my dream of becoming a major league baseball player was not coming to fruition. I hated them for what they were doing to me and I wanted out. I wasn't going to "allow" anyone to do anything to me as I had in the past. I would make my own decisions and steer my own course for what was ahead.

I began to reflect upon everything I had been through since being drafted and although my goal was to become a major league player, I realized that it might not happen. My agent had already reached out to the organization to ask them for my release because other teams had shown a tremendous interest in me, but they had refused – and it was their prerogative to do so. When I sat back and thought about it, I had already proven to myself that I was good enough to play in the major leagues; my constant picks to be on the All-Star teams despite not playing consistently during the seasons also spoke volumes. Sometimes, you can do everything in your power and do everything right and still fall short based on other people's expectations of what "making it" meant. I realized that this may not be for me, but more importantly, I wasn't going to be anyone's victim again or be held hostage mentally as I had been in the past.

When the offseason came, I headed home with a lot of decisions to make, but the biggest one was whether or not I would return to baseball the following season. When I got home, my energy immediately shifted to my family. My family: I had never truly been able to say 'my family' before and have a sense of connection and belonging until then. No matter what my decision would be about baseball, I knew my family would take precedence over everything else.

This offseason was different than any other offseason. I had a new son, Cordell Jr., I had a home and I had a doting wife who nursed my bruised ego from the rough season I had just endured. She had already gone back to work after having our son and, at that point, she was pretty much the breadwinner in the household. When I initially returned, I watched my son as she went off to work each day, but that just didn't feel right, and as a man, I couldn't stand the idea of my wife taking care of the family financially while I sat at home. I knew, though, that working at the YMCA wasn't going to cut it either. For the first time in my life, I had to think about what I would do after baseball. Although I hadn't made a decision about whether I would return, I knew that regardless, it wouldn't last forever. So I began to make the transition personally from baseball, but I was not ready for the change of having to figure out what I was going to do outside of baseball.

I decided to reach out to my former high school baseball coach for some advice. I told him that I would likely give baseball another go for the upcoming season, but that I needed to start thinking about what I would do after that. I knew I enjoyed working with kids, but I wasn't sure in what capacity. As luck or fate would have it, he was now the director of the alternative school in our area and a long-term substitute position had just opened up. He asked me if I was sure this was something I wanted. I assured him it was and I jumped at the opportunity. I didn't know what I was going to do after baseball was over, but this would definitely let me know if teaching would be on my radar when I *was* done.

As it turned out, I really enjoyed working with the young people who, for more than anything else, were misguided. In most cases, they had been expelled or suspended from their home schools and were bussed in from the surrounding counties so that they could continue to get their education. But although I enjoyed working with them, as the time grew nearer for spring training, my energy began to turn back to baseball. I wasn't quite ready to let it go and I knew I needed to go back to give it another shot so that I would have no regrets. My wife fully supported me in my decision and so once again, I headed off for spring training.

When I arrived to spring training in 2001, I was immediately sent to work out in AAA. I felt this was a promising sign, but after a couple of days, they suddenly sent me all the way down to work out in rookie ball with 18 and 19 year olds. I really didn't understand since my workouts had been really solid since my arrival. But they continued to bounce me around within the different levels and at that point, I just knew I was going to be cut – or so I thought.

Over the years, I had garnered the respect and admiration of many of my teammates and they saw what was happening. One of them decided to speak up and ask one of the roving (specialty) instructors where I would be for the upcoming season. To my surprise, he told him that I would be either in AAA or AA. I just didn't get it. If this was the case, why were they bouncing me around?

I didn't have time to become obsessed with why they were making certain decisions. I had made the decision that becoming a major league player was no longer my desire. But I also knew there were a lot of young eyes on me, especially young African-American players who had just come into the organization. I felt compelled to continue to give it my all and see it all the way through until the end. And although I was not one to be vocal, I knew I could lead by example in displaying to them the self-discipline and commitment it would take to rise within the organization.

Chapter 33 ~ The Final Straw

One day during spring training, me and one of the young guys I had taken under my wing were chatting and stretching when one of the coaches/instructors walked over and said rather sarcastically, "What's up?" We both looked at him and asked what was up with him. Then he locked eyes with me and asked again, "What's up?"

I asked what he meant by that question and he proceeded to tell me about what had just transpired in the morning meeting. During the daily morning meetings in spring training, all of the managers reported to upper management the progress of the players from the previous day. This helped them determine who to move up, who to move down and who to cut. The instructor proceeded to tell me that my name had come up and it wasn't in a positive light. He said it had been reported to upper management that I had lazily lagged after a ball that had been hit in my direction in the game the night before. The young player that was stretching with me turned to the coach and said, "He didn't even play in the game the night before." I had known this particular instructor since I had first been drafted and he told me that it didn't sound like me, but he wanted to confront me on it and let me know that it had been reported to upper management.

As he walked away, the other player turned to me and he knew from the smile on my face that I knew it was over for me. I didn't have a snowball's chance in hell to battle with something like that. Upper management goes by what the managers tell them and they were being told that I wasn't putting my all in. It didn't matter that it wasn't' true.

After we finished stretching and tossing the ball around for a while, we headed over to the AA area with the rest of our teammates. The manager huddled everyone around to discuss all of the situations that happened in the game the day before so that we could work on them. The funny thing, though, is that he never mentioned me lagging after a ball. My teammate could see the incredulous look on my face and gently grabbed my arm as if to warn me not to say anything. For a moment, I actually contemplated just letting it go, but then I thought back to all of the other times that I should have advocated for myself and chose not to. I also thought about the rumors I had heard in the past about certain roving instructors not fully disclosing to upper management about my positive impact on the game and my development as a whole. I knew I had to stand up for myself and say something, otherwise, I knew I would regret it.

With the hairs standing up on my back, my voice trembling from anger, I asked him, "Is there was anything else about the game that had concerned you?"

"No," he simply replied.

I decided to push further. "Well, it's my understanding that you mentioned in the meeting about someone lagging after a ball."

He turned to me in a nasty voice and with what seemed to be utter contempt said, "If someone did lag after a ball, they know who they are."

I didn't know where this was coming from, but I didn't care. At that moment, he became the face of every person that had ever wronged me in my life. I completely blanked out. I don't know if I physically attacked him or not, but I do remember lunging at him. The next thing I remember is that my teammates were all surrounding me, attempting to get me to calm down; my shirt was ripped and I had slob flowing from my mouth.

I finally gathered myself and calmed down. I knew this was the end and I was glad I had chosen to end it on my terms. I didn't like the fact that I had allowed myself to be provoked to violence, but I had finally stood up for myself. As I walked away, I heard him yelling that he would make sure I never saw a day in the big leagues. I really didn't give a hill of beans at the moment what he thought he could do to me. No one ever again would have that type of control over my destiny.

When I got back to the hotel, I called my agent, but he didn't pick up. My next phone call was to my wife. I didn't get into much detail, but I told her to get me an airline ticket for the next flight home. We didn't have that type of money to purchase a next day plane ticket, but she didn't object. She could hear in my voice that I was done and that I was ready to come home.

I went to meet with one of the administrators the next day to let him know that I was done. I thanked him for the opportunity the organization had given me and let him know that I would be leaving later that day. I anticipated that he would express to me that the organization had appreciated all I had done for them as well and would be somewhat understanding of what had transpired the day before. Of course, that wasn't the case. He promptly told me that I should leave, especially after the way I had treated his manager and walked out the door without another word to me.

That was the final curtain in my career as a professional baseball player. For a split second, I was sad about what could have been, but I quickly gathered myself and looked forward to the next chapter in my life.

Chapter 34 ~ A New Beginning

As I stepped on the plane that afternoon, I took notice of everything and every movement around me. I knew that this would be the last flight I took as a professional baseball player. I wanted to savor and drink in every feeling in that very moment. I knew I was making the right decision, but the closer I got to the end of the flight, the more unsettled I became. Suddenly, I was no longer locked in on the one thing that had sustained me throughout all the years of turmoil. It was time for my energy to shift to something new in order to support my family and I didn't have a clue as to what I would do. I was ready for the change and I knew I had made the right decision, but the fear of not knowing what would come next almost completely consumed me in that moment.

As a professional athlete, I never really had to worry about getting up and going to work in the real world with the exception of my short gigs during the offseason, and those hadn't really counted in my mind because I knew baseball was always right around the corner. This time would be different, though, and I felt it in every part of my being. But what I also felt for the first time in my life was support. This was a feeling that was new to me as well and it somehow eased the fear that lay within me. No matter what I faced ahead, I knew for the first time in my life I would have the support I had wanted and needed for so many years. My new challenge now was to figure out what to do with the rest of my life. It was a new beginning, but a scary one at the same time, and, for once, I wasn't alone.

Chapter 35 ~ After the Bright Lights

With my baseball career officially over, I quickly realized that I would have to build my own foundation brick by brick in order to become the man, father and husband I wanted and needed to be. My first task was to finish my degree. I had been drafted during my junior year and had not yet obtained my bachelor's degree, so I was ready to jump head first into going to school full time in order to finish as quickly as possible. My wife pushed back on that, however, and reminded me that I wasn't in this thing alone anymore and that I also had a family to take care of now.

We were finally able to make a compromise that worked for both of us. I got a job as a teacher's aide and also did umpiring and baseball camps on the side while I completed my degree. She, in turn, gave me full support in getting all of these things done and also helped me with my schoolwork. Within a year's time, I had completed my Bachelor's degree and accepted a job as a Special Education Teacher. We were building our foundation together brick by brick.

There was still something missing in my life, though, and I just couldn't quite put my finger on it until I started watching my wife interact with her family. I started to long for what my "real parents" were like and wonder how life would have been had I been raised by them. Would I have endured the many things I did as a child? Would I have had sibling interactions like those of my wife and her siblings? So many questions lingered.

Chapter 36 ~ Awakening

My wife began to tell me about the rumors she heard while we were in high school about the identity of my real parents. She told me my mother's name was Beverly and her husband's name was Freddie. Ironically enough, she had actually rode the bus with their children when we were in middle school. She told me the stories of how they would get on the bus most days with disheveled hair and clothes, and how they were often picked on because of their appearance. She described the house they had lived in as small in stature and down a wooded path that could barely be seen from the road. Both of my parents displayed some type of mental disability and the four kids seemed to have some type of marked mental disability as well.

As I reflected on this particular piece of information about the whole family having disabilities, I had an epiphany about my long ago interactions with Big Ma. I now believe that all of her verbal attacks on me and her threats of sending me to the "crazy house" were in direct correlation with her knowledge of my biological mother's limited mental capacity. She knew that she had a mental disability, so she had automatically assumed that I did as well and treated me accordingly.

Another revelation was that my biological parents were dark complexioned, which didn't make sense to me or my wife since I am fair-skinned. So we finally decided to do some research and were able to get a hold of my original birth certificate. It confirmed what she had told me about who my birth parents were supposed to be. We both concluded that although it listed her husband as my father, it was highly unlikely that he really was, given their description and how I didn't look like either one of my supposed parents, especially my father. Maybe this was why they had given me away? I suddenly I had even more questions than answers, but what my wife told me next shook me to my core.

When Latrice was in the eighth grade, she was one of the flower girls at the funeral of my birth parents' older son. This completely floored me. She was a flower girl at his funeral? As the story goes, the father (my purported father) had accidently beat him to death while disciplining him one night. He had a physical handicap in the legs, but he also had some type of underlying heart murmur that had gone undetected, and when his father began to beat him that night, something went horribly wrong. I was in a complete daze as Latrice recalled the funeral and how the father had been arrested, but was allowed to attend the funeral in handcuffs escorted by jailers. After that tragic incident, the remaining children were put into foster care and the mother (my birth mother) moved away to another state with distant relatives. My purported father was sentenced to prison.

I tucked this story away in the back of my mind. I just wasn't ready to deal with the reality of what my life may have been like had I not been taken in by Big Ma and Granddaddy. And although I really didn't have an interest in pursuing any type of relationship with my birth mother or her family, I still wondered who my biological dad could be. My wife and I would often joke that he must have been a white man since I was so fair-skinned and my biological mother was so dark-skinned. We also imagined how awkward it must have been at the hospital the night I was born. Out pops some little light-skinned baby and I'm sure my "father" was saying, 'No way this kid is mine!'

This all made me think back to Big Ma telling me that someone had found me in a trash can. It all made sense now as to how and why that story just may have been true. It was painful, but it was also a reality check as to what may have become of me had I been left in that environment. Questions still lingered, though…

Chapter 37 ~ Saying Goodbye - Invasion of Privacy – Questions Answered

In 2001, Big Ma succumbed to an illness she had been battling. We were in a good place in our relationship when she passed on and as I said before, now that I had certain responsibilities in my life, I had a better understanding as to why she had done some of the things she had done in the past. She was a strong woman who carried a lot on her shoulders in order to provide for the many people that were placed in her care.

Another loss I encountered was that of my sister Mary. Over the years, she and I had come to a much better place in our relationship. She found out much later that she, too, had been adopted. I believe it was a lot harder on her because she had always believed she was Big Ma and Granddaddy's biological child; they had never given her any reason to think otherwise. Sadly, Mary had suffered from diabetes and kidney problems that eventually took her life unexpectedly at the young age of 36. As I mentally prepared myself on the day of her funeral to say my final goodbyes, I had no idea what was brewing on the back end and what I would be forced to deal with face-to-face soon.

Her service was beautiful and serene. I sat back calm and relaxed, listening to all of the many great things people had to say about her and how many lives she had touched in such a short period of time. Immediately after the service, I had gathered my things and was heading to the fellowship hall at the back of the church where the repast was to be held. My wife headed to the bathroom and said she would meet me in the back. As I walked down the narrow hallway at the back of the church, I felt a tap on my shoulder. I just assumed it was someone coming to console me, but before I could turn around, someone else grabbed my wrist and pulled me so close to them that I could barely breathe. She began to sob uncontrollably and was saying something, but I couldn't quite make out what it was. For a split second, I thought it must have been someone Mary knew. Then she stood back and just looked at me as she continued to cry. There before me was a woman who clearly was full of pain and at the same time, for some reason, full of joy.

The words she was saying finally began to penetrate my ears as she continued to rotate between hugging me and staring at me. "My son, my son! After all these years, I finally get to see my son."

Wait, what? Her words dropped on me like a ton of bricks. The very proverbial bricks of my original foundation were plundering before me left and right as I stood there speechless and numb. There stood in front of me the person who had brought me into this world. I was shocked and couldn't really gather any words to say.

As I tried to process what was happening, my wife walked out of the bathroom and the initial look of confusion on her face immediately turned to protective mode when she realized what was happening. I was finally able to snap back into the present moment and quickly handle the situation before my wife and niece's (she had figured out what was happening as well) mamma bear claws started swiping. I turned to Beverly (my birth mother's name) and calmly said, "It's nice to meet you, but right now is not the appropriate time for this." I was grieving the loss of my sister and she needed to respect me and the rest of my family during this time. As she continued to cry, I firmly said, "How about I take your number and give you a call?" She obliged.

Cordell Farley

Chapter 38 ~ Final Question Answered

I didn't initially make that call. What would I say? Why did you throw me in the trash? Were you trying to kill me? What state of mind were you in when you made the decision to give me away or rather throw me away? No, I didn't care about any of the answers to these questions – not at that point in my life. How would they further my growth now as a man? In my mind, they wouldn't, so I didn't ask. I felt absolutely no connection with her that day as we stood in the church and I went with that. The only remaining question I had was who was my real father? And I had a feeling she wouldn't be so quick to share that with me. My guess was that if it was a white man, maybe she had been raped and it would be too painful for her to relive that time in her life. I decided to leave well enough alone…but fate has a way of inserting itself into your life just when you need it.

A couple of years later in a conversation with her mother, my wife was told that a man by the name of Red Top Turner may have been my father. I had never heard of him, but my wife's family had known his family very well. Suddenly, my interest was piqued again and that longing I had felt about where I came from came back stronger than ever. The imaginary person I had built in my head suddenly had a name. When I mentioned it to one of my wife's cousins, it was like a light bulb had lit up inside his brain. He said that the possibility of Red Top being my father totally made sense because my son looked just like him. My son: my flesh and blood looked like someone who could possibly be my father. I was beyond excited to hear this, but that hope was quickly dashed.

Sadly, Red Top Turner had died many, many years before. Apparently, he was much older than Beverly at the time I was conceived. To my knowledge, he never got married and never had any other children. As the story goes, he was a local drunk, but one that had a very proper accent and spoke very intelligently. His mother and father owned many acres of land and were one of the wealthiest black families in town back when not very many black people owned anything. One of my wife's aunts actually worked in their tobacco field as a little girl and Red Top himself was good friends at one point with my wife's uncle.

From all accounts, it sounds like he had the upbringing that I had always longed for: loving parents and a stable home life. The very things it seemed he took for granted, were the very things I would have given anything to have. Red Top had the ingredients to do great things in life, but it appears that he never had the drive nor will to accomplish or pursue them.

I also wonder if he knew I existed before he died. Would things have turned out differently had his parents (my paternal grandparents) known he had a child? The answers to these questions will likely never be answered, but I am at peace. I now have the love and support of my own family, and that's all I've ever really wanted.

Epilogue

"Life Lessons from a Throwaway Kid"

So what are the "life lessons" I have learned from my life as a "throwaway" kid? Many, but here are some of the most significant ones that have helped define and shape who I am today.

LIFE LESSONS

1. Your current circumstances do not dictate your future.
2. Change the way you look at things and the things you look at will eventually change.
3. Even when things aren't going your way, always be prepared because you never know when your number will be called.
4. Use your circumstances to build up your mental toughness.
5. Use life's challenges as stepping stones to build yourself up rather than excuses to lean on.
6. Only God can judge you.
7. God places you where you are meant to be.
8. Nothing that is truly real can ever be threatened.

Cordell Farley

Author Bio

Cordell Farley was born and raised in Blackstone, VA. He graduated from Louisburg College with his Associates of Arts Degree in 1995 and then transferred to Virginia Commonwealth University where he was drafted by the St. Louis Cardinals organization in 1996. Mr. Farley spent his entire career with the Cardinals in their minor league organization. After his career ended, Mr. Farley returned to Virginia to pursue his second passion of educating and inspiring youth.

Upon obtaining his Bachelor's degree in Sociology with a concentration in Special Education from Virginia State University in 2002, he became a Special Education teacher for Chesterfield County Public Schools. He taught middle school for five years before deciding to venture into entrepreneurship along with his wife, Latrice. Together, they have owned several small businesses in sports management, real estate, food service and trucking.

Mr. Farley enjoys spending his time mentoring and motivating young people. He is a big believer in self-education and self-improvement. *Life Lessons of a Throwaway Kid* is his poignant memoir which offers a glimpse into his life growing up as a foster kid in a small town, and how he used sports to triumph over the many obstacles he endured both as a child and, later, as an adult.

Cordell Farley

Farley resides in Chesterfield County, Virginia with his wife and children. The enterprising couple are currently writing a second book chronicling the raw and sometimes comical emotions of a couple navigating the challenging world of business while maintaining a healthy relationship.

*To learn more about Cordell Farley, please visit: cordelldfarley.wix.com\cordelldfarley. To schedule an interview with Cordell Farley, please send an email inquiry to: latricefarley@aol.com.

Follow Cordell on Social Media
Facebook – www.Facebook.com/CordellFarleySr
Twitter - @CordellFarleySr
Instagram – cordellfarleysr

Life Lessons of a Throwaway Kid

By Cordell Farley